TWAYNE'S WORLD AUTHORS SERIES

A Survey of the World's Literature

Sylvia E. Bowman, Indiana University

GENERAL EDITOR

AUSTRALIA

Joseph Jones, University of Texas at Austin

EDITOR

Henry Kendall

TWAS 387

Henry Kendall

HENRY KENDALL

By W. H. WILDE
University of New South Wales

TWAYNE PUBLISHERS
A DIVISION OF G. K. HALL & CO., BOSTON

Library of Congress Cataloging in Publication Data

Wilde, William Henry.
  Henry Kendall.

  (Twayne's world authors series ; TWAS 387 :
Australia)
  Bibliography: p. 169 - 75.
  Includes index.
  1. Kendall, Henry, 1839 - 1882 — Criticism and
interpretation.   I. Title.
PR9619.2.K4Z93   821   75-41479
ISBN 0-8057-6229-9

Contents

99543

About the Author

William H. Wilde, M.A., Dip. Ed., M.A.C.E., is a graduate of Sydney University and is a Senior Lecturer in the Department of Language and Literature, Faculty of Military Studies, University of New South Wales. His research interests are largely in Australian literature, particularly in the poetry of the nineteenth century. He is the author of *Three Radicals* (1969) in which he considers the Australian poets, Bernard O'Dowd, "Furnley Maurice" (Frank Wilmot) and Dame Mary Gilmore. He is also the author of *Adam Lindsay Gordon* (1972) in the Australian Writers and their Work series. At present, in collaboration with Professor T. Inglis Moore, he is preparing the authorized biography of Dame Mary Gilmore and is editing a selection of her letters.

Preface

Writing in the *Melbourne Review* in October, 1882, only two months after Henry Kendall's death, Alexander Sutherland, something of a literary expert of the day, expressed the hope "that a few of Kendall's pieces will find their way into Australian schoolbooks, and so become known to the rising generation," for he, along with many others, believed Kendall to be the first real poet to have "woven the beauties of Australian skies and seas, rivers and mountains, into verse." Sutherland has had his wish but Kendall's reputation as a poet has not been well served in the process. "Bell Birds," "September in Australia," and "The Song of the Cattle Hunters" are among the most frequently anthologized of Australian poems for schoolchildren; and Kendall has come to be known and judged as a poet by a handful of minor poems out of his whole life's work. "Kendall for sweetness"; Australia's "Morning Star of Song"; poet of "sweet and melancholy confidences" — such labels, inspired by the popular lyric poems named above, and others like them, have confined Kendall to the narrow literary niche of sentimental lyrist, where he has languished, while lesser Australian poets have been rated above him.

There has been a growing feeling in recent years that Kendall's reputation as a poet ought not depend solely, or even to a major degree, upon the landscape lyrics. Indeed the quality of his lyric poetry is now, itself, in question. A rigorous critical evaluation of it (not a pleasant task since one is dealing with old favorites) reveals that, for generations, critics have taken Kendall's lyric talent too much for granted. It is much less a talent than has hitherto been thought. An unfortunate result of the continued emphasis on his lyric poetry has been the neglect or dismissal of other areas of his work and a consequent ignorance of his wider poetic skill.

In my analysis of Kendall I have attempted to weigh each area of his poetry, from the romantic and "native Australian" poetry of his early period, to the painful, autobiographical lyrics and the satirical poems of his final years. When all of Kendall's poetry is examined closely it is clear that there is so much more to him than the traditional assessment of melancholy lyric poet that one is compelled to turn aside from a century of established opinion and conclude, as I have done here, that Kendall has made a much larger contribution to Australian poetry than has usually been acknowledged. And this contribution has come, not merely from the one controversial area of his lyric poetry, but from his work as a whole.

Such a conclusion is not, of course, unique. In 1957, T. Inglis Moore pointed to the considerable merit of Kendall's narrative poetry; T. T. Reed's meticulous collection of Kendall's poetry in 1966 gave Australians the opportunity to see and judge for themselves the quality of *all* of the poet's varied work; the recent selection of Kendall's writing by Leonie Kramer and A. D. Hope, published in 1973, has been especially valuable in directing attention to his lesser known poetry, and it must be instrumental in inspiring a fresh burst of enthusiasm for him. I acknowledge my debt to these authorities on Kendall and express my thanks for the pleasure which their work has given me. I also acknowledge a particular personal debt to Right Reverend T. T. Reed, recently retired as Archbishop of Adelaide, for allowing me to browse among his Kendalliana and for giving me access to his unpublished thesis for the degree of Doctor of Letters at the University of Adelaide in 1953. Without his research, a labor of love for over a quarter of a century, this work on Kendall would have been infinitely more difficult and far less pleasurable. I am also grateful to Donovan Clarke for permission to consult his unpublished thesis entitled "A Critical Edition of the Letters of Henry Kendall." The librarians and staff of the Barr Smith Library, University of Adelaide; the Fisher Library, University of Sydney; the Mitchell Library in Sydney; the National Library in Canberra and the Bridges Memorial Library of the Royal Military College, Duntroon, Canberra, have been of assistance in allowing me access to Kendall material and I have appreciated their help. Miss Sue Bessell and Miss Pam Capsticks, who have had the responsibility for typing this manuscript, have been magnificent and I am greatly indebted to

Preface

them. My colleagues Grahame Johnston, Barry Andrews, Ridley Bryan, John Laird and Joy Hooton have been cooperative, sympathetic, encouraging, as and when the need arose. Finally, as always, my gratitude to my wife Ena for her patience and encouragement . . . sine qua non.

W. H. Wilde

Duntroon, Canberra.

Chronology

1839   Henry Kendall born near Ulladulla, South Coast of New South Wales.

1852   Kendall's father dies of tuberculosis in Clarence River District, North Coast of New South Wales.

1855   Kendall, aged sixteen, goes to sea on Joseph Kendall's brig *Plumstead.*

1857   Returns to Sydney. Sets up home for mother, brother, three sisters.

1859   First poem, "Oh, Tell Me Ye Breezes," published in the *Australian Home Companion and Band of Hope Journal.*

1861   Friendship with J. Sheridan Moore and J. L. Michael.

1862   Correspondence with fellow poet Charles Harpur begun. Publishes *Poems and Songs,* his first volume of poetry.

1863   Clerk in Surveyor General's Office. Acquaintance with Henry Parkes begun.

1866   *The Bronze Trumpet,* a satire, published anonymously.

1867   Romance with Rose Bennett.

1868   Marriage to Charlotte Rutter. Pressure from financial and domestic problems. Deaths of Michael and Harpur.

1869   Daughter Araluen born. Leaves Sydney for Melbourne. Publishes *Leaves from Australian Forests,* his second volume of poetry.

1870   Araluen dies. Cantata (words by Kendall) sung at opening of Melbourne Town Hall. Kendall, in debt and alcoholic, returns to Sydney. First son, Frederick Clarence Kendall, born.

1871   Treatment in Gladesville Mental Asylum for addiction and melancholia.

1872   Mental and physical breakdown, referred to by Kendall as "The Shadow of 1872."

1873   Further treatment in Gladesville Mental Asylum. At Gosford, late in the year, in care of Fagan family.

1874   Remains at Gosford working for Fagan timber mills and attempting to overcome alcoholism. No contact with family.

1876   Reunited with wife and family at Camden Haven. Alcoholism overcome.

1879   Submits winning poem for Sydney International Exhibition.

1880   Publishes *Songs from the Mountains,* his third and last volume of poetry.

1881   Appointed Inspector of Forests, Cundletown, N.S.W.

1882   Dies in Sydney, August 1. Buried in Waverley Cemetery.

CHAPTER 1

The Life of Henry Kendall

H ENRY KENDALL'S paternal great-grandfather is the earliest of the poet's ancestors who can be traced with certainty.
He was Laurence Kendall, a middle-class Lincolnshire farmer in the
latter part of the eighteenth century. The poet's grandfather,
Thomas Kendall (Laurence Kendall's son), was born in Lincolnshire
in 1778, ten years before the First Fleet arrived in Botany Bay.
Thomas Kendall's hectic and colorful life is an epic in itself. As a
young man in England he tried farming, school teaching, shopkeep-
ing and speculation in the hops market before going to New Zealand
as a lay missionary and school teacher. After many doubtful es-
capades he was suspended in 1823, in Reverend Samuel Marsden's
opinion, "a public disgrace to the sacred ministry."[1] In 1825 he left
with his family for Valparaiso in Chile where he had been offered the
post of clergyman to the British residents there and tutor to the
British Consul-General's children. In 1827 he returned to New South
Wales to take up a grant of 1280 acres of land in the Ulladulla district of the colony's south coast. The Ulladulla grant contained some
valuable stands of cedar which Thomas Kendall felled and
transported to Sydney on a small cargo ship, *Brisbane*. In August,
1832, the ship capsized in a storm off the mouth of the Shoalhaven
River and all hands, including Thomas Kendall, were lost.

I *Kendall's Parents*

The poet's father was Basil Kendall, the second son of Thomas
Kendall. Basil Kendall was born in England in 1807, spent his
boyhood in New Zealand and went with his parents to Chile as a
young man of eighteen. He served as a junior officer from 1825 to
1827 in the Chilean Navy and then followed his parents back to New
South Wales. For the next few years he worked in Sydney as a clerk.
On August 1, 1835, he married Melinda Olivia Leonora McAllan —

13

such was the name recorded on the marriage certificate. The origins and background of this woman, who was to become the poet's mother, have proved difficult to verify. Charles Swancott, historian of the Brisbane Water country and interested in the poet Kendall because of his connection with that area, said that the string of mellifluous names was a pure invention.[2] He claims that Basil Kendall's wife's real name was Melinda McNally, the name which is recorded on her death certificate. Archbishop T. T. Reed believes her to have been Matilda McNally, the daughter of Patrick McNally, an Irish policeman who had been stationed in Sydney but who later went on to a grant of land near Wollongong in New South Wales. Archbishop Reed's opinion upsets the theory that the poet's mother was the daughter of the well-known Irish barrister and playwright, Leonard McNally. Whatever her origins — and her real name — Henry Kendall's mother was aged twenty at the time of her marriage to Basil Kendall. Their beginnings were not auspicious. An infant, Mary Kendall, was buried in Sydney in October, 1835, the year they were married. For about two years Basil and Matilda remained in Sydney, attempting a living by selling victuals and other supplies. They went in July, 1837, to settle on a portion of the Ulladulla property, known then as Kirmington, about two miles from the present township of Milton.

II *Early Life*

In a slab hut on the property, Henry Kendall and his twin brother Basil Edward were born on April 18, 1839. The poet was baptised Thomas Henry Kendall by a Presbyterian minister on July 26, 1840. Biographical inaccuracies about Kendall's Christian names and his date of birth persisted for many years. Both 1841 and 1842 were given as the year of his birth by biographers in the middle and late nineteenth century, these dates being based upon unsubstantiated statements by either the poet or his wife. One such statement occurs in a letter that Kendall wrote to the editor of the *Cornhill* magazine on January 21, 1862, indicating that he was then in his nineteenth year.[3] It seems, in retrospect, that Kendall was hoping to obtain a more generous assessment of his poetry from the *Cornhill* critics by giving an impression of extreme youth. Contemporary critics, accepting the *Cornhill* letter as evidence of his age, perpetuated the error. A similar whim accounted for the appearance of the Christian names "Henry Clarence" on Kendall's marriage certificate in 1868. He had spent two periods on the Clarence River at Grafton — in the 1840s and again in the early 1860s. Perhaps he adopted the name to record his affection for the place; a more likely explanation is that to an imaginative young man attempting to make his way in the literary world "Clarence" seemed more romantic and poetic than the plebeian "Thomas Henry" of the baptismal record.

The circumstances surrounding the departure of the Kendalls from Ulladulla after seven years are rather obscure. Neither Basil nor Matilda was temperamentally suited to the arduous and lonely farming life; both were periodic alcoholics. Matilda in particular having a reputation among Basil's brothers, Edward and John, as "a bad lot." Archbishop Reed points to the depressed state of rural industries in the early 1840s as an additional cause of their leaving the land. In 1844 they were back in Sydney. Basil resumed his former occupation as a clerk and they lived apparently on South Head Road. On January 3, 1848, Basil was found guilty of forging and uttering and sentenced to two years jail.[4] On his release he took his family to a sheep property named "Gordon Brook" on the Clarence River near Grafton. After a year they moved to another sheep run, "Bushy Park," on the banks of the Orara River about eight miles from the Grafton township; and finally they moved into Grafton itself where Basil, for a short time, conducted a school. Henry Kendall passed the impressionable years of his boyhood on the Orara and the Clarence and he dug deeply into his memories of those scenes and experiences in his later poetry. On September 23, 1852, Basil Kendall died of consumption, leaving his wife and five children (there were three girls, Christina Jane, Mary Josephine and Edith Emily) in difficult circumstances. He had not proved a successful father and provider, being weak-willed and impractical. Henry later described him as a "mild, gentlemanly and educated man" but "an indifferent man of business. . . . He was always speculating but he died poor." There is a note of affection and very little bitterness in these reflections by the son many years after his father's death. He attributed much of his education to his father's influence and was grateful on that account. His relationship with his mother was deeper. Between them was an affinity that her embarrassing vagaries and indiscretions stretched painfully but never fully destroyed. She was a "Currency Lass" — "pretty, witty Tilly McNally" — with an Irish combination of charm, devilry and appetite for life quite untempered by any self-restraint. Her legacy to her poet son was twofold — a tempestuous and charming, though weak, nature and a lively Celtic imagination and love of literature. Kendall wrote of her: "From her I inherited what talents I have. At the age of nine I was introduced by her to the then current translation of Homer and I took a genuine boy's delight in that book; and in Bunyan's stalwart hero, Greatheart. Every bush I came across was either an Achilles or a giant."[5] After the father's death the family depended on the charity of relatives. They returned to Sydney where the mother and the twin boys went to live with her father, Patrick McNally, on his farm at Fairy Meadow near Wollongong while the girls were arranged for at boarding schools and with other relatives. Henry may have spent a year or so at Ulladulla with his uncle Edward before joining his mother and brother at Fairy Meadow. The years from 1852 to 1855 were described by him later as "illiterate and friendless" years.[6] In poetic terms they were to be, however, remarkably fruitful. He had returned to the natural beauty of that southern coastal plain where he had been born. The Illawarra district would have been in those days quite unspoiled, a natural paradise, and echoes of its sights and sounds fill Kendall's earliest poetry.

In 1855, when he was sixteen, he went to sea aboard his Uncle Joseph's brig, *Plumstead,* a whaling vessel of less than two hundred tons. The brig did not return to Sydney until March, 1857. The two years Henry spent at sea were clearly unhappy, although in later years he wrote an idealized account of a fictitious voyage through the South Seas to the Antarctic regions. His wife, his son Frederick C. Kendall, and his friend Joseph Fagan have all indicated that these were days Henry preferred to forget. There were hints of hard times with physical punishment and uncomfortable conditions.

Back in Sydney he reunited the scattered family. His uncles sold a parcel of the Ulladulla land — probably Basil Kendall's share of the estate — and the money provided a home for Matilda and the children, first at Camperdown and later at Newtown, Sydney. Henry worked for his uncle Lawrence Kendall, a miller and biscuit maker in the city, then for a confectioner at Newtown, and afterwards for Biddell Bros., sweets manufacturers of Brickfield Hill.

III   *First Poems*

On February 26, 1859, two months before Kendall's twentieth birthday, his first poem was published. Four attractive little verses entitled "Oh, Tell Me Ye Breezes," pondering the fate of the explorer Leichardt who had vanished in the great Australian emptiness, appeared in the *Australian Home Companion and Band of Hope Journal.* There is conflicting evidence about possible earlier poems than this slight lyric. Kendall claimed to have written "The Ballad of Tanna," a romantic legend of the island of Tanna in the New Hebrides group, while on the *Plumstead* voyage, that is, in about 1856 or 1857. Archbishop Reed has observed, quite reasonably, that the "Tanna" poem displays such a superior technique to the other examples of Kendall's early work that it was probably not written until just before its publication in the *Sydney Morning Herald*, July 11, 1861. "The Merchant Ship," a long poem about the sinking of the *Dunbar*, which cost 121 lives in 1857, was said by Kendall to have been written at the time of the wreck but it did not appear in print until published in the *Empire*, March 8, 1860.

The *Empire* provided an outlet for Kendall's early poetry. By the end of 1860 it had published twenty-one poems and he was beginning to attract the attention of literary personalities. His friendship with Joseph Sheridan Moore, teacher, poet, journalist and critic began as a result of the *Empire* poems. It was, at first, mainly a literary patronage but it deepened with the years into a strong personal attachment. Moore's combination of literary expertise and business acumen was invaluable to Kendall. He encouraged Kendall to publish his first volume of poems by a subscription edition, a commercially sound arrangement whereby many copies are bespoken before their publication and financial risk to the poet, or his publisher, is minimized. The *Empire* and the *Sydney Morning Herald* carried in January, 1861, the following advertisement:

THE MUSE OF AUSTRALIA — In preparation for Publication (by subscription), THE POEMS AND SONGS OF HENRY KENDALL, the boy-poet of Australia. At the request of several literary and influential gentlemen, and after a severe critical examination of the work, MR. SHERIDAN MOORE has consented to superintend the publication. So convinced is he of its merit that he has no fear of commending it to the taste and patriotism of the country. *Subscription Lists lie at several book and music dealers, in town and country.

The newspaper advertisements were augmented by a printed leaflet in which Moore said of Kendall's poems:

I have submitted several of them to the judgment of two of the keenest critics in the Australian colonies, who have both approved of them in the promptest manner and most encouraging language. In hope, Sir, that you will cheerfully patronise home genius when it develops in such beautiful

forms as it does in HENRY KENDALL'S POEMS AND SONGS, I offer no
apology for asking you to become a subscriber to the work now offered to the
public.

With Moore as his mentor Kendall's circle of friends and acquaintances was widened and improved. It included Nicol D. Stenhouse, a
lawyer and competent classical scholar, Dr. John Woolley, Principal
of the newly founded University of Sydney and Daniel Deniehy,
politician, orator and scholar. Henry Halloran, a senior civil ser-
vant and dabbler in poetry, offered. Kendall a clerical position
in the Surveyor-General's Office but he preferred the more ex-
citing prospect of a personal and working relationship with James
Lionel Michael, a Sydney lawyer and poet. Michael had come to
New South Wales in the Gold Rush days of 1853, but, preferring the
comfort of the city to the rough life of the diggings, he remained in
Sydney to set up a legal practice. A poet of some talent (*Songs
Without Music*, 1857), a man of considerable culture, learning and
personal magnetism, his influence on Kendall was not completely
wholesome. Kendall benefited in many ways — he quit his draper's
job to do part-time clerical work for Michael, at first in Sydney and
later in Grafton; he had free access to Michael's fine library; he improved his own limited education by instruction from and discussion
with Michael; he was given both encouragement and the necessary
leisure to write as much as possible. There were also some less
beneficial aspects of the friendship: Michael's judgment and
behaviour were inclined to be erratic, his temperament unstable, his
way of life not always above reproach, and Kendall's own nature
blended far too easily with a combination such as this. They were not
close friends for long, although there was never an open breach
between them, but the friendship came at a time when Kendall
would have been better served by a less volatile relationship.

IV   *Correspondence with Charles Harpur*

It was in the same period that Kendall's relationship with Charles
Harpur began. His letters to Harpur (excerpts of which are discussed
more fully in Chapter 5) give a poet's eye-view of the contemporary
social and literary scene and attempt a well-meaning scrutiny of the
other's work. In an early letter, September 25, 1862, just after he had
returned from Grafton to Sydney to supervise the production of his
first book of poems, Kendall sought the development of their
friendship. He wrote:

I am very anxious to correspond with you; being assured that mentally I shall gain much by your letters. For we cannot leave a cedar grove without carrying away some of the fragrance. . . . I feel already deeply indebted to you for the great good and large comfort I have derived from your writings. . . . There is no living author to whom I could turn and say as much. This may be a necessary result of my Australian birth and education. . . . I have always looked upon you as the man who alone could express what I had so often dimly thought.

The correspondence flourished, with Kendall the more regular writer. They did not meet personally until December, 1867, more than five years after they first exchanged letters and some six months before Harpur died, June, 1868. Kendall volunteered to act as Harpur's literary agent in Sydney and although they were, in a sense, literary rivals, he did his best to publicize Harpur's poetry and to increase the pitifully small public regard for him.

V *Some Personal Problems*

In October, 1862, Kendall's first collection, *Poems and Songs*, was published by J. R. Clarke of Sydney in an edition of five hundred copies, 369 of which were sold before the publisher went insolvent. In 1864, Kendall, believing the book to be a failure, tried to suppress the remaining hundred or so copies. The poems were, on the whole, generously received. The *Sydney Morning Herald* declared "Mr. Henry Kendall is a poet of much promise" while other reviewers judged that "the poems are the best yet produced by any son of the soil. . . . Young Henry Kendall is a born poet" and "Henry Kendall's lately published volume . . . is full of rich promise."[7]

Shortly after *Poems and Songs* appeared Kendall approached Henry Halloran for a Civil Service position and was appointed as Extra Clerk in the Survey Offices. His position was made permanent on January 1, 1864, at a salary of 150 pounds a year. Although his family life was stable at this time his financial affairs became hopelessly entangled — a state they were to remain in for many years. His salary was small, but reasonable, and it is difficult to know the true cause of his money problems. He blamed his family's extravagances, while claiming that his own habits were moderate, even frugal; however, later, when he was free of his family, he managed his affairs no better. His letters at this time are filled with complaint and self-pity, the querulous, whining tone of some of them being utterly distasteful in a young man of twenty-five. In a letter to the editor of the

London *Athenaeum*, February 17, 1866, he grumbled, "In my spare hours and whenever health and the choking troubles of a really hard life have suffered me I have written and written on." He complained that he was not receiving proper recognition for his literary achievements and began to play outrageously upon these to win promotion in the Civil Service.

His prime target was Henry Parkes who had become Colonial Secretary at the beginning of 1866. On January 25, 1866, Kendall wrote to him: "I do not like to take advantage of your present position by assailing you with more applications for your influence in my favour. But there are others to be considered and I must make a sacrifice of my delicacy . . . I believe the few friends of Australian literature now left would be very grateful to you for any kindness you might bestow on me."

In April he borrowed twenty-five pounds from Parkes and being unable to pay the final five pounds payment in October he borrowed a further five pounds. In December, 1866, he received promotion in Parkes's own department at a salary of 250 pounds, yet he continued to seek loans from Parkes and others. Correspondence indicates that as late as 1869 he still owed Parkes thirty pounds. In seeking patronage to advance in the Civil Service Kendall was merely following long-established practice and should, perhaps, not be judged too harshly for that. It is more difficult to excuse his widespread borrowing from friends and acquaintances.

During these years of young manhood Kendall was in and out of love on several occasions. He did fall deeply in love with Rose Bennett, the daughter of Samuel Bennett, proprietor of the *Empire*, but the romance did not prosper. A. G. Stephens of the *Bulletin* believed them to have been engaged early in 1867 but to have parted as a result of a lovers' tiff.[8] Other evidence indicates that Rose Bennett preferred another literary man, John Henniker Heaton, whom she later married. The sonnet "Laura" (originally entitled "Rose"), published in the *Australasian* June 16, 1869, and a twin poem, "By A River," published a few days earlier in the same newspaper, express Kendall's feeling for Rose, the "marvellous maid" of the "ripe red mouth and luxurious eyes." The wistful love song, "Rose Lorraine," which closes his second volume of poems, *Leaves from Australian Forests*, and the bitter "At Nightfall" clearly mark Rose Bennett as the lost but never-forgotten love of his life. On September 17, 1867, Kendall, by then well-known in Sydney's cultural circles, delivered a lecture at the School of Arts on the subject of love. After the lecture he met Charlotte Rutter, the eighteen-year-old daughter of a deceased Sydney doctor, John Rutter. They became friendly and the relationship deepened into courtship. Six months later, on March 7, 1868, they were married and moved into a cottage owned by Mrs. Rutter in Glebe. Soon after the marriage his problems with his own family grew more irritating. His youngest sister was secretly married; expenses were incurred by his mother and sisters for which he was allegedly held responsible; his twin brother forged his name on a cheque for forty-five pounds which Henry paid to save the family from unwelcome publicity; household furniture which he felt was rightly his was supposedly given to his sister's new husband, whom he regarded as a rogue. These complaints were all made sometime later in a letter of June 22, 1869, to Dr. J. E. Neild seeking (rather typically) "the loan of three or four pounds on my promissory note for say three months." Some of his accusations against his family seem exaggerated and it is possible that his list of woes and his additional lament — "At present I am actually ill. Scholarship does not go for much down here" — were intended to soften the heart and loosen the purse strings of Dr. Neild.

The year 1868 brought the deaths of J. L. Michael in Grafton and Charles Harpur at Eurobodalla. Kendall wrote a sincere tribute "James Lionel Michael" which J. Sheridan Moore included in his memorial *Life and Genius of James Lionel Michael*, 1868, and "Charles Harpur," a memorial poem which was printed in the *Sydney Morning Herald* July 7, 1868, together with a lengthy obituary notice of the dead poet. In the memorial poem is Kendall's judgment that Harpur was the first great poet to tune "the Harp Australian." Kendall's own most notable poem of 1868 was "A Death in the Bush" which won the *Williams's Illustrated Australian Annual* competition for the year. It was a poem, which, in the assessment of R. H. Horne, the judge of the competition, could only have been written by one "who has made Poetry and the Poetic Art . . . the ruling passion of his life."[9]

VI *Melbourne Episode*

After Parkes's departure from the Colonial Secretary's Office in September, 1868, Kendall lost his patronage and became exposed to the hostility of fellow employees. His relationship with his wife's family was not cordial. His financial affairs were as chaotic as ever. He took leave of absence from his position between July and October, 1868, to visit Melbourne to investigate the opportunities there for a writer, and subsequently resigned from the New South Wales Civil Service on April 1, 1869. He left for Melbourne where he was soon joined by his wife and infant daughter, Araluen, then three months old.

The Melbourne episode was a complete disaster. Kendall contributed at times to the *Australasian*, the *Argus*, the *Australian Journal* and other newspapers, but was paid little for his efforts; he persuaded the Melbourne publisher George Robertson to print his second volume of poems, *Leaves from Australian Forests*, but it failed to sell in spite of quite favorable reviews; he tried, mostly unsuccessfully, to get other literary work. As bad times turned to worse he began to drink heavily. His self-respect and will power gradually crumbled. He moved with his wife and child from poor lodgings to even poorer ones, in suburbs progressively lower down the social scale. His young wife bore much of the brunt of this decline. She pawned their few possessions for money to pay the rent and to buy food. The money Kendall received for his spasmodic work went mainly on alcohol. Araluen, at first a bright, healthy baby, became seriously ill. She died February 2, 1870, and was buried, according to some accounts, in a pauper's grave, in the Melbourne General Cemetery. Years later the memory of these Melbourne events was expressed in the wretched, painfilled verses of "On A Street" and "At Her Window."

Dr. Neild, the drama critic of the *Age* and the *Argus* and a prominent member of the Melbourne medical profession, befriended Kendall and through the Yorick Club brought him into touch with other literary figures such as Marcus Clarke, George Gordon McCrae, Adam Lindsay Gordon and J. J. Shillinglaw. Hugh McCrae's father, George Gordon McCrae, who published a short biography of Kendall a year after the poet died, has provided a description of him at that time:

He was a man about middle height, spare and thin but quite the reverse of athletic. He was pale and somewhat wrinkled, and the expression of his countenance as a rule sad. His hair which was crisp and curly (latterly of an iron grey color) he sometimes trimmed but never cut; in fact when I first knew him it used to conceal the collar of his coat. His cheeks were naturally bare but he wore a small, rather sparse looking beard tho' his moustache in after years was quite a heavy one. His eyes were of a blue-grey tint, but changeable, and lighting up to a perfect blue as he became animated in conversation. Nervous to a degree, he never felt at home unless he happened to have something either to touch or to hold, and many will remember the manner in which he used to embrace his umbrella as he conversed with them. His dress was invariably black — a frock suit with a tall black hat chiefly remarkable for the narrowness of the brim. Though good natured and amiable to a fault, he was nevertheless ready and quick to take offence. In fact, being a Poet, he was over-sensitive and too often was apt to fancy malice where nothing but fun was intended . . . .What he most loved were quiet saunterings or rambles in the country with a friend, but though he invariably shortened the road by his brilliant talk he was not what is known as a clubable gregarious man. Perhaps, as I have thought sometimes, he preferred solitude even to the best of company.[10]

Kendall does not appear to have been a social success at the Yorick gatherings but occasionally (usually after a glass or two of brandy) he threw off his shyness and participated in the Yorick discussions to some effect — "once he began to talk none but a fool could affect contempt. The Lord God put a soul in him, and that soul burned his tongue and lightened through his eyes."[11]

Kendall and Adam Lindsay Gordon, kindred spirits in some ways, had a brief relationship in those months of 1869. They spent some time together on June 23, 1870, discussing the bleak prospects that faced the man of letters in the colony. One story, impossible to corroborate, is that they had seven shillings between them and spent it drinking most of the afternoon away at the Adam and Eve Hotel in Little Collins Street. If the story is true (Archbishop Reed is one who doubts it) then they would not have been good company for each other. Gordon had received that morning, from his publishers, his new booklet of poems, *Bush Ballads and Galloping Rhymes*. He was in debt to Melbourne moneylenders because of expenses incurred in his vain attempt to prove his claim to the old Gordon baronetcy of Esslemont in Scotland and the publishers' account increased his troubles. The next morning Gordon shot himself on Brighton Beach. Hugh McCrae tells of Kendall writing a note to his father, G. G. McCrae, revealing his inability to attend Gordon's funeral because he did not have the money to get to the cemetery. The note Kendall wrote to G. G. McCrae was addressed to A. L. Gordon, esq. but that name had been crossed out and McCrae's substituted. Whether the error had been due to grief or drink is difficult to know. The note read: "Dear Gordon: at 4 p.m. this afternoon I haven't the money to spare, or I would attend. Indeed I am penniless. Yours truly, Henry Kendall." Hugh McCrae comments: "This must remain one of the most poignant letters ever written. A letter to the dead."[12] A week after Gordon's death the *Australasian* carried Kendall's poetic tribute, "The Late Mr. A. L. Gordon: In Memoriam."

VII *Further Personal Difficulties*

Kendall had been commissioned to write a cantata for the opening of the new Melbourne Town Hall on August 9, 1870.[13] For this work — "Euterpe: An Ode to Music" — he received about eighty pounds, sufficient to take his wife, expecting another child, and himself out of the Melbourne misery back to Sydney where Mrs. Kendall had at least the refuge of her family. They arrived in Sydney October 24, 1870, but very little in their lives had changed, Kendall still drinking most of what he could earn. On November 25, 1870 he was committed for trial on a charge of forging and uttering. The amount was trifling, one pound, but he was brought to trial on December 21, 1870, defended by W. B. Dalley and acquitted on the grounds of temporary insanity. A few days later, December 24, 1870, his first son, Frederick Clarence Kendall, was born and his wife left him to live with her mother. It seems hard to blame her for this action. She was then only twenty years old and had known with Kendall two years of extreme mental and physical anguish. His further deterioration after she left him did not occur without painful efforts on his part to resist his weaknesses, but on July 5, 1871, he was admitted to Gladesville Lunatic Asylum suffering from a mixture of alcoholism and over-use of opiates, probably in the form of sedatives, and as a result of these, extreme depression and melancholia. The Asylum records describe him as "worn, thin and ill." He was discharged some three weeks later. It was said by the hospital authorities that "he feels his position acutely and is most anxious to continue his literary work for the sake of his wife's support."[14] He contributed frequently, after his discharge, to the *Freeman's Journal*, conducting a regular feature "The Harp of Erin" and writing feature articles entitled "Men and Books".

The following year, which he always referred to afterwards as "The Shadow of 1872," is largely unrecorded. Occasional documents or letters, and in later years a number of poems, are grim evidence of the events of that year and early 1873. Incidents such as a missed appointment with Henry Parkes — "I was too ill yesterday to wait upon you. I am suffering from dysentry and face ache"[15] — and a request for a loan from P. J. Holdsworth — "Can you (being a

brother in the arena of literature) raise me half a crown to take me
over the day?"[16] — tell their own story. He worked on casual journalist jobs, gained money for drink wherever and whenever he
could, and wandered Sydney's streets little better off than the other
drunks whose gutters he sometimes shared. "The Shadow of 1872"
remained in later years blurred and confused in his memory. "I
recollect very little of my subsequent Sydney life; for my mind was
unhinged nearly all the time."[17]

In April, 1873, he was readmitted to Gladesville Asylum. By then
he was seen, in the Asylum's medical report, as "extremely nervous
and in a depressed condition of mind and body. . . . He is sleepless
by night and morbid and melancholy by day. He is very emaciated
and pale." There is a poignant echo of his guilt over Araluen's death
in the doctor's comment — "He imagined that he was accused of
murdering a child."[18] He remained under treatment for more than
two months. During this period his friends were busy and by the
time he was discharged from Gladesville they had gained for him
editorship of a Grafton newspaper. They outfitted him and paid his
steamer fare from Sydney to Grafton. Kendall went, as they wished,
but his heart was not in it. He had had enough of writing, blaming
his literary talent and its inability to sustain him and his family for
much of the misfortune of the past. He hoped, vainly, for a reconciliation with his wife and family, a second son having been born. At
Maitland, 100 miles north of Sydney, he left the ship, spent the
refunded portion of his steamer fare on drink, sought and failed to
find casual journalist work, then set out to return to Sydney on foot.

VIII   *Rehabilitation at Gosford*

After several days of walking, interspersed with an occasional ride
from fellow travellers, Kendall reached an inn at Wyong Creek.
There he met Charles Fagan, Justice of the Peace and Truant
Inspector from the Hawkesbury River to Morisset. Two of Fagan's
brothers had a timber business in Sydney and were exporting cedar
from the Gosford district to America. The rest of the Fagan family
lived at Gosford on the banks of the Narara Creek (then Narrara),
one of the many beautiful streams running into the Brisbane Water,
the northeast arm of Broken Bay. It was there that Kendall was taken
by Charles Fagan to repair the mess that his life had become. In an
incredible gesture of compassion and understanding the Fagan
family took the hapless poet under their care and he spent the next

two years living in their comfortable old stone house beside the Narara. After several weeks of rest and care Kendall's health began to improve but the ghost of alcoholism was to take a tremendous amount of laying. By October, 1874, however, he could write "I have taken nothing stronger than tea for the last eleven months."[19]

For almost a year Kendall dropped out of existence. Neither his wife nor his family knew of his whereabouts and he had little information about them. By June, 1874, his location was known to P. J. Holdsworth and the two corresponded about some of Holdsworth's poems. Then his old friend, J. Sheridan Moore, got in touch with him. Suggestions that he resume writing were for some time refused or ignored — "Nothing shall tempt me to write for money again; and the life I have chosen precludes me from writing for pleasure."[20] He became a surprisingly effective timber-man. When not working in the Fagan store as a storekeeper and accountant he visited the sawmills around the district, checked the quality of the cedar they were milling, bought what was suitable, measured and tallied it and arranged for its transport to the Fagan timber yards in Sydney. He swam, rode and worked until his restoration was complete. There was a touch of the miraculous about his mental and physical recovery. Few men are able to come back from the brink as he had done and his success dispels any doubts as to his moral fibre. It says much also for his good friends, the Fagans. The customary image of him as weak-willed and self-indulgent clearly needs reappraisal in the light of his struggles at Gosford.

Kendall welcomed the contact with the old world that Holdsworth's and Moore's letters gave him but, embarrassed about his past, he remained anxious that his whereabouts be kept secret. His thoughts turned increasingly toward an eventual reconciliation with his wife and children. He still maintained that she had deserted him when he needed her most, but his attitude did her less than justice, and Kendall must have known this in his heart. When the supplies of cedar at Brisbane Water began to run out, the Fagans established a new mill at Camden Haven, about 250 miles north of Sydney. Kendall accepted their offer to go there as accountant and storekeeper. It meant a new start, with fresh hopes, so in September, 1875, Mrs. Kendall agreed to join him; there was, however, no suitable accommodation for her. The Fagans, anxious to help, built a house for him at Camden Haven and toward the end of 1876 they were reunited.

IX *Last Years*

The final, fruitful, peaceful period of Kendall's life began at Camden Haven. But it was no leisured, bucolic existence that he followed: "Our business here is a large and flourishing one: and I have an aptitude for it which sometimes is a source of astonishment to even myself . . . my time is nearly all engrossed by worldly work . . . business swallows up nearly every moment. . . . There is no Sunday in this obscure part of the bush. . . . I have to work very hard: too hard indeed to admit of much flowerage and outcome in the way of belles lettres."[21] There were two saw mills each employing twenty to thirty men, and half a dozen coasters were continually engaged between the mills and Sydney. The district had two centers: that at which Kendall and the Fagans resided (now called Kendall after the poet) and Laurietown. In his few spare hours Kendall now began to write, in a new style, satirical verses on political and topical subjects. These proved popular with the newspapers who could not get enough of them. Generally he wrote under pseudonyms, "The Mopoke," "Tiresias," "The Meddler," "A Literary Hack." He was still ashamed about his past and the pseudonyms were one way of avoiding attention. Writing to Henry Halloran on October 2, 1878, he commented " . . . my past will not bear analysis and I always dread its being raked up." The new family life was harmonious. The tensions of the old days gradually dropped away, suspicions and doubts quietly evaporated as the placid months went by. He delighted in the company of his children and he spent as much time as he could with them exploring the district and initiating them into the loveliness of the countryside. A son, Athelstan, was born in 1877 and two more daughters in the following years, Evelyn Persia in 1878 and Roma in 1879.

Insistent voices from the past kept urging him back to serious poetry. Moore, Holdsworth, Halloran and G. G. McCrae wrote frequently, always with the same plea. W. B. Dalley (who had defended Kendall against the fraud charge in 1871) felt that Kendall was the right person to compose an ode which could be set to music and sung as a cantata at the opening ceremony of the International Exhibition to be held in Sydney in 1879. Kendall was finally won over. He completed the first draft of the cantata in only a week, his promptness being an indication of his esteem for Dalley as well as his pleasure at once more undertaking a worthwhile poetic task. He won also the *Sydney Morning Herald*'s competition for "a poem to fitly

celebrate the opening of the forthcoming International Exhibition."
The cantata and his prize poem restored Kendall immediately to his
position of prestige in Australian poetry. The *Sydney Morning
Herald*, in publishing the poem, September 17, 1879, declared what
had then not been said for more than a decade, "Mr. Kendall has
long been known as one of the first of Australian poets." Encouraged
by his success he began compiling his third volume of poems, *Songs
from the Mountains*. It was published in December, 1880, but was
withdrawn from sale immediately because the publisher, William
Maddock, feared a libel action over one poem, "The Song of Ninian
Melville." After a new poem, "Christmas Creek," was substituted
the volume was released. *Songs from the Mountains* was aimed to
catch the taste of the general public more than his earlier volumes
and it sold well, Kendall making a profit of about 100 pounds.

Kendall, who had grossly insulted Sir Henry Parkes in 1879 with a
satirical poem "The Gagging Bill," now suddenly appealed to him
— as he had done years before — for a remunerative government
position. The arguments were much the same as twenty years before,
the prose a little more embellished:

I do not wish you to take any step inconsistent with the high character of
your office. It is very many years since I last asked a public man to assist me;
and only the touching plea on young dependent faces makes me do so now.
On behalf of my children, — in the interests of their noble mother, I ap-
proach, not the titled statesman, but the man of letters whose sympathy for
letters is still a warm breathing fact; and ask him — the head of an
Australian Government — to aid, in the way indicated, the first *native* who
has with any degree of emphasis stamped his name upon the poetic
literature of Australia.[22]

The first reaction of Parkes must surely have been one of disbelief.
By October, however, he had put less generous thoughts aside and in
writing to the Attorney General, James Watson, October 7, 1880,
commented: "As you know he [Kendall] has in the past treated me
with cruel ingratitude. But what remains of life for me is too short to
entertain ill-will towards any one." By April, 1881, Kendall had the
position he desired — Inspector of Forests at a salary of 350 pounds
per annum. He moved with his family to Cundletown on the lush,
majestic Manning River. Under the terms of his appointment he was

to inspect and report generally upon the present state of the Forests of the
Colony . . . also to report upon the present system of conserving Timber and

supervising timber-getting, and of collecting the revenue arising from permission to cut Timber etc., and to make such suggestions for the amendment
of the Regulations relating to the management of the Forests and Timber
lands as may appear to you expedient . . . report upon the necessity for, or
advisability of making provision for the renewal of our natural Forests, or for
establishing nurseries and planting out the most useful descriptions of
Timber trees in suitable localities.[23]

These duties were particularly onerous, necessitating constant
travelling, long hours of report-writing and endless frustrations
because of administrative delays and lack of decision in matters
where commercial interests were at variance with forest husbandry
and conservation. His comments to George Gordon McCrae — "My
life is a rather trying one, it is the same as a blackfellow's . . . I am
always on the move" — and to Charles Harpur's widow who was
seeking his assistance in the editing of Harpur's poems — "the out-
door hardship is immense"[24] — reveal the physical difficulties of his
new position. From May to August, 1881, Kendall was inspecting
the state forest in the northern Richmond River area. A serious bout
of illness climaxed this trip and after his recovery at the end of
September, 1881, he confined himself to inspection of Central Coast
reserves nearer his home. But the deterioration in his health continued. He recovered a little over the Christmas-New Year period of
1881 - 82, then went to Sydney in January, 1882, prior to undertaking an arduous and prolonged inspection, mostly on horseback, of
inland forests in the Central Western and South Western areas of the
state. On his return to Sydney early in April, 1882, he was very sick.
After a break of about three weeks he resumed this inland tour but
was unable to complete it. By early June he was so ill at Wagga
Wagga that his friend George Fagan was summoned and with his
assistance, Kendall returned to Sydney to be admitted on June 18,
1882, to St. Vincent's Hospital suffering from phthisis. By the end of
July his condition had worsened considerably and he was, at his own
request, moved from the hospital to Fagan's house in Redfern where
Mrs. Kendall looked after him. There he died on the afternoon of
August 1, 1882. Two days later he was buried in the Waverley
Cemetery overlooking the Pacific Ocean. Gradually the feeling grew
that his passing had been inadequately marked and that some more
significant memorial should be established over his grave. After four
years his body was moved to a more impressive site in the cemetery
and a monument erected. It bore an inscription and two lines from
Shelley's "Adonais":

Here lies Henry Kendall, poet: born 18th April, 1841: died 1st August, 1882. Some of those who loved and admired him have, in grateful and lasting remembrance of his genius, built this monument above his ashes.

Awake him not! Surely he takes his fill
Of deep and liquid rest, forgetful of all ill.

CHAPTER 2

Kendall's Poetry:
The Early Period

K ENDALL was the most prolific of the Australian colonial
poets. He published three volumes of poetry; *Poems and
Songs*, 1862, containing forty-five poems; *Leaves from Australian
Forests*, 1869, fifty-seven poems; and *Songs from the Mountains*,
1880, thirty-five poems. He wrote at least another 180 miscellaneous
poems and some fifty prose articles, most of which were published in
contemporary newspapers and journals. In the three published
volumes can be traced the development of his poetic talent from
young manhood to maturity as well as the range and diversity of his
poetic themes. Although the uncollected poems are, in general, inferior to those of the three volumes some of them are interesting in
that they reinforce — and occasionally vary from — the attitudes
and characteristics of the collected poems. In a critical analysis of
Kendall's poetry it is both convenient and logical to keep broadly to
the general chronological order of the three volumes.

I   Poems and Songs

By the time *Poems and Songs* was published in October, 1862,
Kendall had written the forty-five poems included in that volume
and some thirty-six other pieces most of which had appeared in print
between 1859 and 1862. Of the forty-five poems of his first volume,
only four, "Mountains," "Stanzas," "The Barcoo" and a brief
tribute "To Charles Harpur" had not already been published in
local newspapers and journals.

Kendall preserved, in a Scrapbook now in the possession of
Archbishop Reed, several complimentary contemporary reactions to
Poems and Songs:

There is a certain fitness about this book, looked at as a specimen of printing,
and its contents or soul. The poems are the best yet produced by any son of

the soil and the book itself is the best of printing produced here. Young
Henry Kendall . . . is a born poet. All his writings are free and flowing, and
there is no appearance of effort about them. He does not, like some we
know, manufacture verses by a slow and painful process, but they leap out
from 'the study of his imagination', warm, breathing, full of life and
permeated with the fire of his genius.[1]

Now we have young Henry Kendall, who has just published a book of songs.
Many of our readers must have observed short poems in the newspapers by
this young singer and must also have been struck at the vast command of
language he possesses. His language is highly descriptive and graphic, and
he has the faculty of word-painting largely developed. He is also delightfully
fresh in spirit — sings with a jocund air, and seems to revel in the beauties of
our mother nature, which dull eyes pass by unnoticed.[2]

The stale assertion that Australia has produced no one who may rank with
the 'glorious brotherhood', simply betrays a rash conclusion . . . who, after
reading Henry Kendall's lately published volume — so full of rich promise
as it is — can doubt the rising of another poet among us? We feel sure that
these men [Charles Harpur had also been mentioned] have not only
faithfully pictured the beauties, but have caught the very spirit of our
scenery . . . surely such poems as "The Barcoo," "The Song of the Cattle
Hunters," "The Wild Kangaroo" and "The Wail in the Native Oak" will
become national.[3]

Such praise must be weighed against the tendency of some contemporary critics to overvalue colonial writing. Kendall himself was later
dissatisfied with many of these first poems. The Mitchell Library
holds a copy of *Poems and Songs* (apparently purchased years
afterwards in a secondhand book shop in Sydney by Henry Lawson)
which Kendall has inscribed:

Author's Revised Copy. I have in this copy made the alterations which are to
be adhered to in all future editions of the poems altered. Many of the pieces
are struck out. Let them be forgotten. Platitudes and Pleonasms won't 'go
down' with Readers even in Australia: I was very young then when the
following pages were published. There is much in them that I now ignore;
and much that may always be remembered by me gladly. They are the
sincerest records of dead emotions.

There are few poems in this first volume that could be considered
among the best of Kendall's poetry. They carry, as they must, the

stamp of his inexperience — both of the art of poetry and of life itself. They are interesting, nevertheless, in that they are, as he has said, the record of his youthful emotions and they reveal his early efforts to formulate the literary and philosophic attitudes which are the basis of his maturer work.

There is, for example, abundant evidence that Kendall's chief literary ambition, at the age of twenty-three, was to be a "Native Australian Poet," one whose poetry was deeply rooted in the Australian environment. Many of these early poems thus attempt to reflect the spirit and character of Australian life and to picture the beauty of the Australian landscape. They range from descriptions of the coastal countryside to narratives of colonial life to outbursts of patriotic pride in the country's rapid movement toward nationhood. Running through them is a strong sense of the "spirit of place," the young poet's reaction to his environment.

Poems and Songs also reveals Kendall, at twenty-three, as the traditional young romantic, very much attracted toward ideal human relationships and strongly inclined to melancholy. Two clear themes emerge from the many intimate, personal poems of the volume — the possibility of a life beyond this life, free of imperfections, unhappiness and sorrow (Kendall's concept of "Aidenn"); and the need for a perfect human relationship (especially an ideal love relationship between man and woman) to provide security against the hazards and uncertainties of life. Thoughtful and imaginative young poets have always been preoccupied with such matters and have been stimulated by that preoccupation into absorbing, though often depressing, intellectual and emotional analyses. It is almost inevitable that a pensive, rather mournful note should emerge as the characteristic tone of poetry which probes such themes. The presence of this melancholy note in Kendall's early poems led critics to label him "a very dolorous poet."[4] The melancholy was to persist throughout his life, accentuated by the sombre events of that life and by his own pessimistic disposition. Of poets in general and himself in particular he wrote:

Men and women, with the poetic temperament, are generally sorry creatures: if their sense of enjoyment is keen, their sufferings are extreme. They seem to live a two-fold life; constantly over-balanced, and surrounded by exaggerations. In my case, I have enough of that *acute* sensibility to work myself into a constant flutter with excitement. And therefore depression of spirits is, with me, the rule, and momentary elevation, the exception.[5]

Poets are, as it were, *cursed* with a peculiar temperament which renders
them wholly vulnerable to that peculiar fiend, *Melancholy*.[6]

The first poem in the volume is "The Muse of Australia,"[7] printed
originally in the *Sydney Morning Herald* August 28, 1862. It is Kendall's own judgment of the quality of this, his first poetry, and his in-
tuition of the future:

> Where the pines with the eagles are nestled in rifts,
> And the torrent leaps down to the surges,
> I have followed her, clambering over the clifts,
> By the chasms and moon-haunted verges.
> I know she is fair as the angels are fair,
> For have I not caught a faint glimpse of her there;
> A glimpse of her face, and her glittering hair,
> And a hand with the Harp of Australia?
>
> I never can reach you, to hear the sweet voice
> So full with the music of fountains!
> Oh! when will you meet with that soul of your choice,
> Who will lead you down here from the mountains? —
> A lyre-bird lit on a shimmering space;
> It dazzled mine eyes, and I turned from the place,
> And wept in the dark for a glorious face,
> And a hand with the Harp of Australia!

Kendall's poem owes something of its origins to Harpur's "The
Dream by the Fountain." In Harpur's poem "a lofty-souled Maiden
. . . the Muse of the evergreen Forest" appeared to the poet in a
dream. She touched the strings of her lyre:

> Divine were the measures! Each voice of the wildwood
> Seemed gathering head in their musical thrills —
> The loud joy of streams in their strong mountain childhood,
> The shouting of Echoes that look from the hills:
>
> The moaning of trees all at midnight in motion,
> When the breezes seem lost in the dark, with a rare
> And sweet meaning spirit of human devotion,
> All blended and woven together were there!

Her playing ended, the Muse spoke to the dreaming poet, offering
him glory — "Be then the Bard of thy country!" He wakes, certain
of his destiny: "I know that 'tis mine 'mid the Prophets to stand!/No

matter how many that blame be anear me,/I feel like a Monarch of Song in the Land!" Kendall's poem carries the opposite certainty, that it is not he who is destined to be the great national poet of the future, unveiling in his poetry the true glory of the land. Not for him the Muse's loving words to Harpur, "I am the Spouse of thy spirit, lone Bard!" He can never be ". . . that soul of your choice/Who will lead you down here from the mountains." Forty years later, when the cult of nationalism sought to crown an Australian king of song, whatever claims were made on Kendall's behalf were brushed aside by the accusation that his poems were un-Australian in description, character and sentiment. Kendall's own denial of his right to the position is based here simply upon the quality of his poetry, upon the plain fact that he was not an inspired poet. His unhappy complaint to the Muse, "I never can reach you," is followed by the shattering admission of his lost poetic cause. The goal is there, real and desirable, but for him unattainable: ". . . I turned from the place,/ And wept in the dark for a glorious face,/And a hand with the Harp of Australia!" The literary worlds of both the colony and England believed that the young poet had made a promising start. His own judgment, however, was clearly a source of deep and private grief to him. It is remarkable that this early poem from a poet starting out on his poetic career should be so devoid of hope, yet seventeen years later, in the last poem of his final volume, he ruefully confirms his earlier assessment. In "After Many Years"[8] he looks back on his life's poetic achievements:

> The song that once I dreamed about,
> The tender, touching thing,
> As radiant as the rose without —
> The love of wind and wing —
> The perfect verses to the tune
> Of woodland music set,
> As beautiful as afternoon,
> Remain unwritten yet.
>
> But, in the night, and when the rain
> The troubled torrent fills,
> I often think I see again
> The river in the hills,
> And when the day is very near,
> And birds are on the wing,
> My spirit fancies it can hear
> The song I cannot sing.

These poems, so many years apart, confirm the charge of melancholy and pessimism that was so often levelled at him. He seemed a poet without confidence, without hope; aware of the heights of poetic beauty, he was convinced he could never reach them. Yet of the poets of the period he and Harpur were the only ones with some real capacity for greatness. In a lifetime of poetry he had only the briefest flashes of optimism, seldom wanting to think of the future, which he always viewed pessimistically.

There is at all times a mellowed beauty associated with the sunsets of yester-day, which we do not find in the noon of to-day, and cannot anticipate for the morn of tomorrow. To-day is too real for us; tomorrow is too mythical for us. But yesterday is for ever like an eloquent background in a noble picture. And therefore, I think, we see clearest and sing sweetest when our thoughts are with the sobered lights and shadows of the days and nights of the past.[9]

"The Muse of Australia," with its prediction of his failure to achieve the poetic goals that his spirit sought, emphasizes (and may partly account for) the melancholy shadow that darkened so much of his life and work.

II   *The Young Romantic and "mystic Aidenn"*

Edgar Allan Poe had published *The Raven and Other Poems* in 1845, almost twenty years before Kendall's *Poems and Songs*. "The Raven" tells of a lover who mourns his lost love, Lenore. On a bleak December midnight as he vainly seeks to extract from his books "surcease of sorrow — sorrow for the lost Lenore" he hears a tapping on his door. He opens it and a raven enters, perching on a bust of Pallas above the door. To the questions and comments of the bemused poet the "ghastly, grim and ancient" bird utters only the one word "Nevermore." The burning question that Poe puts to it is the possibility of his reunion in another life with his beloved:

'Tell this soul with sorrow laden if, within the distant Aidenn,
It shall clasp a sainted maiden whom the angels name Lenore —
Clasp a rare and radiant maiden whom the angels name Lenore.'
                                        Quoth the Raven, 'Nevermore'.

Kendall took up in his early poems this theme of "Aidenn," a world beyond this world, an Eden paradise beyond the mountains, a land of "unknown shores," "undiscovered skies," "cliffs and coasts by man untrodden" and "shipless seas"; a dream world where lost

hopes, lost loves might be recovered. Linked with the theme of
"Aidenn" is the young poet's vision of romantic love, embodied in
the figure of a lost maiden who has passed from this world to the
"Aidenn" paradise. From there she beckons invitingly to him but
never confirms the certainty of the bliss she appears to be offering. A
prey to doubt and indecision, the poet is left "lamenting to pursue
his empty life on earth."

These themes, though clearly linked to Poe's "The Raven," especially by the borrowing of the word "Aidenn," are not unusual, as
indicated earlier, for an imaginative, sentimental and romantically
inclined young poet, as Kendall then was. Nor are the melancholy
tones in which they are uttered at all surprising. Most young poets'
ponderings on life and love are tinged with melancholy. Such poetry
is, in fact, often the product of the poet's enhanced sensitivity which
renders him more susceptible than most people to gloomy doubts
about the prospects of love and happiness. The theme of Eden is
present also in Harpur's "The Tower of the Dream," not published
until 1865 although Kendall was aware of it in 1863.

Glimpses of the faraway Eden are given in "Mountains," "Fainting by the Way," "Footfalls," and "Athirst." The best expression of
it is in "Mountains."[10] The mountains constitute a barrier both
physical and spiritual; behind them the poet imagines his paradise:

Underneath these regal ridges — underneath the gnarly trees,
I am sitting, lonely-hearted, listening to a lonely breeze!
Sitting by an ancient casement, casting many a longing look
Out across the hazy gloaming — out beyond the brawling brook;
Over pathways leading skyward — over crag and swelling cone,
Past long hillocks looking like to waves of ocean turning to stone;
Yearning for a bliss unworldly, yearning for a brighter change,
Yearning for the mystic Aidenn, built beyond this mountain range.

The "Lovely Being" of "Aidenn" paints a comforting, nostalgic picture of the dreamland and the poet seeks assurance from her that if
he reaches it his cares will vanish, his hopes be fulfilled:

Lovely Being, can a mortal, weary of this changeless scene,
Cross these cloudy summits to the land where man hath never been?
Can he find a pathway leading through that wildering mass of pines,
So that he shall reach the country where ethereal glory shines;
So that he may glance at waters never dark with coming ships;
Hearing round him gentle language, floating from angelic lips;

    Casting off his earthly fetters, living there for evermore;
    All the blooms of Beauty near him; gleaming on that quiet shore?

Like Poe's inscrutable Raven, Kendall's "Lovely Being" refuses such
assurance. He has to decide whether to leave this world for the
"evanescent vision" of that "fair Utopia" or whether to make a
meaningful existence here. He is sad that "the lovely Dream has
flown" but cannot completely commit himself to pursuing it. In his
indecision there is some sign of Kendall's awareness, even in these
early years, that man ought to decide in favor of reality. In several of
these first poems this ambivalence is present. His commitment to the
concept of "Aidenn" is never finally or totally made — tempting and
enticing though it be.

    The situation in "Footfalls"[11] parallels that of "Mountains." In this
poem, and in several others, notably "Bellambi's Maid," "The Maid
of Gerringong," "Aileen", "Watching," "Waiting and Wishing"
and "Geraldine," there appears the haunting figure of a maiden from
whom the poet has been separated by death or time or distance. She
takes several forms. At times she is a tangible, lovely girl like
Geraldine with whom he walks hand-in-hand among the
wattle; more often she is a spirit-girl, like Aileen, "a glittering form
that would not stay," or a "lovely phantom" like the maid of
Gerringong, or a "restless ghost" like the lost love of "Watching." In
"Footfalls" the maiden has died and the poet seeks from her the
answer to the mysteries of "Aidenn." With its emphasis on the
sorrows of this life rather than the joys of the future paradise it is one
of the more melancholy of these early poems:

        Come out of your silence and tell me if Life
        Is so fair in that world as they say;
        Was it worth all this yearning, and weeping, and strife
        When you left it behind you today?

        Will it end all this watching, and doubting, and dread?
        Do these sorrows die out with our breath?
        Will they pass from our souls like a nightmare, I said,
        While we glide through the mazes of Death?

Again, like Poe's tormented lover, Kendall is left unsatisfied: "You
answer me not when I know that you could — . . . And my heart is as
cold as your grave."

    The situation where lovers are parted is best illustrated in "The
Maid of Gerringong,"[12] a sensitive and perceptive analysis of how

the human spirit should cope with the problem of lost love. The poem begins by recognizing that love offers an initial fleeting ecstasy that soon gives way to apathy or a long anguish. In either case there follows a keen sense of loss. This loss, however, is never total. Life will have been so enriched by love that even in the dead or lonely years that follow, gleams of its remembered beauty will remain. Two anodynes for the lover's aching heart are offered, one illusory and the other real. Since man must face reality the recapturing of lost love by reverie or dream is shown to be spurious, doomed to failure. The only true reunion will be in death, "the coming Morning" in "Aidenn," when the lovers will recover their lost rapture and then possess it forever. This is the consolation that the "lovely phantom" maid — her tears of parting significantly described as "radiant" — offers her lover to overcome his grief at their parting:

Said my darling, looking at me, through the radiance of her tears:
'Many changes, O my loved One, we will meet in after years;
Changes, like to sudden sunbursts flashing down a rainy steep —
Changes like to swift-winged shadows falling on a moony deep!
And they are so cheerless sometimes, leaving, when they pass us by,
Deepening colours on the sweet sad face of our Humanity,
But you'll hope, and fail and faint not, with that heart so warm and true,
Watching for the coming Morning, that will flood the World for you'.

In the empty years after their parting the forlorn lover seeks other men's opinions. One questions, "Can ye love in age as fondly as we did in days of youth?" But another tells him "Love is love, and never dies." Aware at last of the true meaning of the maid's parting words he exultantly replies:

. . . Ay, for Love is Love in Death.
Oh! the Faith with sure foundation! — let the Ages roll along.
You are mine, and mine for ever, dark-haired Maid of Gerringong.

The final part of the poem shows what happens to the dreamer who tries to refashion in fantasy the love experience that has passed by. In dreams the lover pleads with the phantom maid. To his cry "turn and stay, my darling, stay!" she is silent, then fades into the sunset "and the sunset passed from sight." Man cannot simply close his eyes and imagine that all is as it was before. The truth is, as Gatsby found, that you cannot repeat the past and man must build his life on reality, not on illusion.

The poem is a thoughtful, mature judgment by a young man who

had, at the time it was written, only his instinct for life to guide him
— an instinct which has often been judged, reasonably enough on
the evidence of much of his poetry, as inordinately gloomy and
despondent. "The Maid of Gerringong" is certainly not a happy
poem, not even optimistic, but there is an undertone of composure
and assurance running through it. It understands the apparent transience of love and how that transience can result in human pain and
grief. But it points to the deeper significance of love: it can remain,
paradoxically, a source of solace even after it has gone. It is easy
enough, as the world knows, to fashion a philosophy for others, but
much more difficult to follow the path oneself. Kendall was to know
from love far more of the agony than the ecstasy but he did come, in
the end, to find some of the security and certainty that this early
poem predicted.

"Aileen,"[13] whose sensuous pictures of rest and ease in an idyllic
setting remind one strongly of Tennyson's "The Lotos Eaters,"
shows how obsessed Kendall's young mind was by the dream of an
ideal love:

You Spirit of a darling Dream
Which links itself with every theme
And thought of mine by surf or stream,
In glens — or caverned glooms.

"Stanzas"[14] opens with the same note of longing:

The sunsets fall and the sunsets fade,
But still I walk this shadowy land;
And grapple the dark and only the dark
In my search for a loving hand.

The climax to these tortured thoughts of love and life are the lines
"Waiting and Wishing"[15] Man's desire for fulfilment through love
throbs through the poem:

I loiter by this surging sea,
Here, by this surging sooming sea,
Here, by this wailing wild-faced sea,
Dreaming through the dreamy night;
Yearning for a strange delight!
Will it ever, ever, ever fly to me,
   By this surging sea,

> By this surging sooming sea,
> By this wailing wildfaced sea?
>
> I know some gentle spirit lives,
> Some loving, lonely spirit lives,
> Some melancholy spirit lives,
> Walking o'er the earth for me,
> Searching round the world for me!
> Will she ever, ever, ever hither come?
>   Where the waters roam,
>   Where the sobbing waters roam!
>   Where the raving waters roam!
>
> All worn and wasted by the storms,
> All gapped and fractured by the storms,
> All split and splintered by the storms,
> Overhead the caverns groan,
> Gloomy, ghastly caverns groan! —
> Will she ever, ever, ever fill this heart?
>   Peace, O longing heart!
>   Peace, O longing, beating heart!
>   Peace, O weeping, weary heart!

"Kiama,"[16] published originally in the Kiama *Examiner*, May 7, 1861, (lending some credence to the theory that Kendall was then in the district) shows this fulfilment through love achieved. Together, the poet and his bride, watchers on the cliff, look down upon the sleeping little coastal town and the moonlit ocean. It could be — in essence it was — a world of threat. The glory that hovered about the landscape was "mournful," the waves that were breaking on the shore muttered "sounds of woe," the lone ship far out at sea pursued a fragile way, "a vessel walking in her sleep," but the poet from the security of his shared love experiences none of this menace:

I hear a music, inwardly,
That floods my soul with thoughts of joy:
. . . .
The soul that speaks from gentle eyes,
And joy which slips
From loving lips,
Hath made this spot my Paradise!

The situation in the poem is, of course, imaginary. Kendall was neither married nor in love, but so personally assured is the tone (a rarity in Kendall) that one is able to gauge the great significance he attached to love at this time; which is nothing new or remarkable for a young man in any age, and especially for a young poet!

III *Native Australian Poet (N.A.P.): The Spirit of Place*

Kendall sought to create a definite Australian atmosphere as the background for his early poetry. Even the fantasies on love, just mentioned, were set on several occasions against the Australian coastal landscape with which he was so familiar. In other poems he selected activities and aspects of life which he felt had distinguishing Australian characteristics. These attempts emerged, in the main, as fairly traditional English descriptions but they did contain some recognizably Australian flavor. Given the time, the mid-nineteenth century, and the colonial cultural dependence on England, it is presumptuous to expect more.

Several poems of the first volume are alive with this 'spirit of place.' In preparing *Poems and Songs* Kendall revisited, with his twin brother Basil Edward, the haunts of his earlier years, partly to recapture the sense of identity he had known with that lovely South Coast landscape but also to ensure that his poetic reconstruction of it would be as authentic as possible. They are said to have revisited in 1859 and 1860 such places as Ulladulla, Kiama, Wollongong, Gerringong, and Jamberoo. Henry stayed at Jamberoo for some time, managing a store owned by a William Allen and writing some of the poems included two years later in *Poems and Songs*. Four poems carry South Coast names — "Kiama, "Bellambi's Maid," "Wollongong," and "The Maid of Gerringong." "Wollongong"[17] is reminiscent in tone, recapturing the gratification of youthful senses drugged by the beauty of long summer days spent roaming along golden sea shores, in cool moist gullies, on green headlands where sky and ocean blended in a dazzling blue and white world:

Here we rested on the grasses, in the glorious summer hours,
When the waters hurried seaward, fringed with ferns and forest flowers;
When our youthful eyes, rejoicing, saw the sunlight round the spray
In a rainbow-wreath of splendour, glittering underneath the day;
Sunlight flashing past the billows, falling cliffs and crags among,
Clothing hopeful friendship basking on the shores of Wollongong.

There is local colour also in "Bellambi's Maid."[18] The star-crossed lover laments where "The tall mimosa spreads its locks/Of yellow hair, to hide the glade" and where

> The foggy peak of Corrimal,
> Uplifted, bears the pallid glow
> That streams from yonder airy hall
> And robes the sleeping hills below.

In "Kiama" the setting is not especially important, the cliffs of Kiama being irrelevant to the poem's theme of security in love, but the choice of the title is indicative of Kendall's desire to link his poetry to the Australian environment. Most of the romantic love poems have a common setting — beetling cliffs which lead onwards to a lonely shore and a restless surf, and backwards to deep-shadowed gullies, cool forests and green ridges, all components of what has come to be accepted as the typical Kendall country. They are not however, landscape poems. Kendall's longing for love provides the focus of the poems, the landscape serving only as a backdrop against which these longings are expressed. The use of the local landscape in these early poems is, nevertheless, the beginning of a pattern which was to be repeated in much of his later poetry.

Three hunting poems in this first book also attempt, but with only limited success, to capture the 'spirit of place,' the atmosphere of the Australian bush, and its associated activities. "Wild Kangaroo"[19] begins on an exuberant note more associated with an English fox-hunt:

> Oh, ye who are fond of the sport,
> And would travel yon wilderness through,
> Gather — each to his place — for a life-stirring chase,
> In the wake of the wild Kangaroo!
> Gather — each to his place — for a life-stirring chase
> In the wake of the wild Kangaroo!

Kendall's fellow colonials, Adam Lindsay Gordon and Charles Harpur, experienced much the same difficulty in creating a true Australian atmosphere. They were still searching for the right words to use, for the Australian idiom, as we know it, was then largely un-formed. Harpur's long poem "The Kangaroo Hunt or A Morning in the Mountains," an attempt at an Australian "pastoral," is thoroughly English in tone, the local flavor coming only in the copious footnotes attached to it. In Gordon's "The Sick Stockrider" too, when the hunt is for bushrangers and lives are at stake, the action resembles a game played by high-spirited young English gentlemen clad in elegant riding habits and mounted on splendid thoroughbred horses. In "Wild Kangaroo" Kendall has only a smattering of the local color — the shepherd's dog (which in a later slip of the pen becomes the more English word 'hound'), the bell bird and the kangaroo itself. The infusion of atmosphere from these small details is not sufficient to make the poem as natively Australian as Kendall had probably hoped. The second hunting poem, "The Oppossum Hunters,"[20] was first entitled (in the *Empire*, June 9, 1862) "Opossum Hunting by Moonlight, A Bush Ballad." It has a rousing ballad rhythm but even less than "Wild Kangaroo" to distinguish the setting as the Australian bush. The use of the expression "bush ballad" is interesting for it indicates that Kendall had the germ of the idea which is said to have sprung into life with Gordon's "The Sick Stockrider" but which was not properly born until the publication in the *Bulletin*, Christmas 1889, of a poem "Clancy of the Overflow," signed by someone calling himself "The Banjo." "Banjo" Paterson's later volume, *The Man from Snowy River and Other Verses*, 1895, brought the bush ballad to its peak of development.

The final hunting poem, "The Song of the Cattle Hunters,"[21] is one of the best-known and widely recognized 'Australian' poems of the volume. Together with later verses such as "Bell Birds," "September in Australia," "The Last of His Tribe" and "Bill the Bullock Driver," it has been responsible for placing Kendall among what Americans would term "the school room poets." Published in the *Empire* on September 2, 1861, and later praised by the London *Athenaeum*, it gives only the barest glimpse of an activity that is characteristically Australian (and quite un-English) — the hectic fury of a cattle roundup. The poem has a trace of historical interest if it is accepted as one of the earliest examples of Australian "galloping rhymes." It is more poetic than the usual "galloping rhymes," however, attaching itself far more readily to Tennyson's "The Splendour Falls" than to the rough and ready, easygoing bush songs of the Australian balladists. Together with its two companion pieces, however, it is a refreshing change from the troubled, melancholy, personal poems which are so numerous in this first collection. In it Kendall's lyricism is given a brief freedom from its customary introspective restrictions. It revels in the blur of violent action, man and beast combining in a helter-skelter of crashing movement and explosive sounds which settle back after the impetus of their noisy onward rush into an attractive diminuendo of fading echoes:

While the morning light beams on the fern-matted streams,
And the water-pools flash in its glow,
Down the ridges we fly, with a loud ringing cry —
Down the ridges and gullies we go!
And the cattle we hunt they are racing in front,
With a roar like the thunder of waves;
As the beat and the beat of our swift horses' feet
Start the echoes away from their caves!
      As the beat and the beat
      Of our swift horses' feet
      Start the echoes away from their caves!

Like a wintry shore that the waters ride o'er,
All the lowlands are filling with sound,
For swiftly we gain where the herds on the plain,
Like a tempest, are tearing the ground!
And we'll follow them hard to the rails of the yard,
O'er the gulches and mountain tops gray,
Where the beat and the beat of our swift horses' feet
Will die with the echoes away!
      Where the beat and the beat
      Of our swift horses' feet
      Will die with the echoes away!

It is one of the earliest examples of Kendall's interest in the lyric possibilities of a stream of mellifluous, rhythmic cadences — attempting, on this occasion, to catch and match the rhythm of flying hooves.

IV *The Australian Shepherd*

Three further poems, similarly filled with the 'spirit of place,' are those which make up the unfinished work "The Australian Shepherd": namely "A Death Scene in the Bush," "The Curlew Song" and "Morning in the Bush." They were all published in the *Empire* during 1860 and the last two were also included in *Poems and Songs*. Kendall appears to have planned a work of considerable size, "The Australian Shepherd," using the sheep herder as the central figure around which to weave the epic story of life in the Australian bush. Since these three "fragments" are the only evidence of this magnum opus, it can only be assumed that he abandoned the task. Kendall probably felt well fitted to write the saga of the Australian shepherds. He had spent several years tending sheep on the Gordon Brook and Bushy Park runs near Grafton when his father was station manager, a grandiose title for duties that were mainly shepherding. In a letter to Henry Parkes in 1863 he stated "... from my eleventh to my fifteenth year I had been following sheep: illiterate and friendless."

The three poems are linked by the presence of the shepherd, by descriptions of his bush environment, and by oblique references to the hazards and hardships that were part of his life. The Australian shepherd, that strange hermit of the bush, with his long beard, his musket over his shoulder instead of a crook, his rough blue serge suit tied at the waist with a leather belt from which there usually protruded a pistol, was a familiar figure in the colony until he was made redundant by the gradual spread of fencing wire over the pastoral areas. A solitary human figure in the vastness of the bush he slept wherever the sheep were pasturing, his only companions his dogs and the flock. On established runs, such as Kendall knew, the shepherd was less nomadic, living, sometimes with wife and children, in a rough slab hut which had a bark roof and a dirt floor.

"The Curlew Song"[22] creates the eerie atmosphere of the bush at night which the shepherd would have known well. There is the moaning cry of the wind in the trees, the midnight howl of the dingo, and the answering bark of the watchdog. Over the whole scene floats the endless, doleful shriek of the curlew, the loneliest, saddest sound of the bush: "They rend the air, like cries of despair,/ The screams of the wild Curlew!" Kendall's clever, repeated use of the long-drawn-out final syllable of the bird's mournful sounding name creates an air of desolate abandonment that is almost unendurable. Some shepherds broke under the strain of this self-imposed isolation. Detached for long months from the company of fellow humans they grew strange and unbalanced, such hopeless misfits when restored to society that they could only return to the solitude that had become part of themselves.

In "Morning in the Bush,"[23] originally entitled "Christmas Morning in the Bush," the scene takes on the more cheerful hues of daylight. The "sleepy dingo" drowsily eyes the busy sun as it climbs above the trees while the mournful curlew calls have given way to the ear-splitting cacophony of the laughter of the "goburras" (the kookaburra or laughing jackass). The landscape, distorted by midnight's shadows into a "wild chaotic heap" of "damp and broken crags," is transformed by the morning sunshine into a "ferny hillside" "Where many a modest floweret grew,/To scent the wind-breaths round," and where the snowy mountain lily, in shy decorum, "like some sweet Oriental Maid," hides its beauty behind earthy ledges and among concealing rocks. Sunlight falls upon the "leaf-strewn water pool" dispersing the mists that had curled over the "dark-faced world" of the curlew's night. Under a shelter of "inter-twining wattles" lies the still-sleeping shepherd while nearby the sheep begin their morning graze among the ironbarks. The whole bush leaps into a riot of life as the full glory of the Australian day unfolds:

> Amongst the gnarly apple-trees,
> A gorgeous tribe of parrots came;
> And screaming, leapt from bough to bough,
> Like living jets of crimson flame!
> And where the hillside growing gums
> Their web-like foliage upward threw,
> Old Nature rang with echoes from
> The loud-voiced mountain cockatoo;
> And a thousand nameless twittering things
> Between the rustling sapling sprays,
> Were flashing through the fragrant leaves,
> And dancing like to fabled fays;
> Rejoicing in the glorious light
> That beauteous Morning had unfurled
> To make the heart of Nature glad,
> And clothe with smiles a weeping World.

"The Curlew Song" and "Morning in the Bush," together with poems such as Harpur's "A Midsummer Noon in the Australian Forest" and "A Storm in the Mountains," show Australian poets at work upon the task of creating the true atmosphere of the bush. Their success was patchy, at best. In the lines quoted above, for ex-ample, the early colonial inability to detach overlaid English at-titudes from observation and description of the local scene is quite evident. But "The Australian Shepherd," and Kendall's adoption at this time of the initials N. A. P. (Native Australian Poet), show that he was at least trying to break away from the old conventionalizing influences.

The most substantial of the three "Australian Shepherd" poems is "A Death Scene in the Bush."[24] This long narrative was published originally in the *Empire*, August 24, 1860, then an enlarged and quite changed version appeared on April 15, 1865, in the *Sydney Mail* under the title "Orara — A Tale." Finally as "A Death in the

Bush," with some 100 lines excised from the *Sydney Mail* poem, it won a prize offered at the end of 1868 by *Williams's Illustrated Australian Annual* for an Australian poem. In that final form it appeared in Kendall's second volume of poetry, *Leaves from Australian Forests*, published in 1869. Because it appeared originally as part of "The Australian Shepherd" it is more fitting to discuss it here rather than later among Kendall's narrative poems. Kendall's use of "Orara" in the title of four poems is confusing. Orara was the name of the river which flowed through the Bushy Park run near Grafton where Kendall had been a shepherd boy. The word itself seems to have come from "Urara," the aboriginal name for that elegant eucalypt of the Australian forest, the spotted gum tree.

In its original form the poem quickly focuses on "A lonely, deep, sequestered spot,/Where, mantled in the moonlight stood/A shepherd's slabbed and bark-thatched hut." It is a calm Australian night; a "ruddy moon" and "cheerful stars" look down with placid unconcern upon the human drama below. The spartan interior of the shepherd's hut is described. It is a "cheerless room" with a damp, cold "plankless floor." A rough wooden table, a bed of straw, crudely made chairs, and some tin utensils are its only furniture. Death is present in the hut, reflected in the now pallid work-worn face of the shepherd. But Love is also there and while it cannot hold back Death it comforts the dying man:

> And hand in hand was pressed the while.
> Some few heart springing tears were shed
> As the woman passed her arm below
> To pillow up her husband's head.
> Then one sad whispered question fell,
> And passed along the sunken cheek
> Of him that heard the loving voice,
> But could not find the strength to speak;
> But firmly yet the hand was press'd,
> And still the taper light would glare
> Across those eyes, as if to show
> The faithful love that lingered there.

Morning light reveals the woman bent, weeping, over her man's body. By midday when the "life-essential radiance" of the sun has sparkled the whole of nature into joyous existence, "a few sad human beings" kneel around the shallow bush grave, pray briefly and pass "like dreams away." The woman sits silently by the grave through the long afternoon into the twilight.

The dying shepherd and his grieving wife are poignantly drawn. They are the strength of the poem, created from life with a realism that gives substance to the events in which they share. In his use of Nature the poet's discretion and judgment are not so skilful. The opening and closing scenes, emphasising Nature's aloof unconcern with man's suffering, are soundly conceived but too elaborately and prettily executed. The most inept area of the poem, where the cloying touch of sentimentality almost ruins the effect of realistic human grief, is when Nature is called to share in, rather than be a detached observer of, the shepherd's death:

> The moon was hid behind a cloud
> That brooded o'er the forest trees,
> Where sad low voices rose and fell —
> The murmurs of a midnight breeze;
> And dreamy whispers from the woods
> In slow succession came, and crept
> Between the chinks, to kiss the face
> And fan the brow of him that slept.
> Then roaming round the silent room
> They lingered where the logwood blaze
> Had faded out beneath the gloom,
> As fadeth hopes of other days.

The second version of the poem, entitled "Orara — A Tale," published almost five years later, retains the central action of the original poem, the death scene in the hut, but is otherwise unrecognizable. Kendall adds an introductory section which sets the events in the Orara River country and gives a melodramatic account of how the shepherd and his wife came to be living their lonely life in the bush. He had been transported because of a false charge brought against him in England by the brother of the "sweet-faced girl" whom he had married against her people's wishes. She had followed him and now they lived in this desolate, inhospitable land (the concept of "exile" being still strong in the mid-century period) with only their love to make life bearable. The second section describes the death of the shepherd in the hut. Kendall's strong sense of "place" seems to have demanded a more characteristic Australian backdrop to this new version of his story. He introduced a bush fire and a violent summer storm and at the funeral of the shepherd the colonial version of the laconic bushman who, not finding words to tell of his sorrow, leaves the grieving woman a bag of tea and the comfort that "God will help you, missus, yet." As if to give the Almighty room to manoeuvre to that effect he immediately seeks his horse "And spurring swiftly, galloped down the glen." Worse follows. The woman returns to England, then one day receives a letter of confession from her dying brother telling of his misdeeds. Her husband's name cleared, she waits for their reunion on hills "that slope through darkness up to God."

This is all much inferior to the first version. The sentimentality, the stereotyped situation of wronged and suffering innocence, the exaggerated use of Australian background events — it has strong echoes of Harpur's "The Creek of the Four Graves" and is, with Harpur's poem, perhaps the beginning of the "flood, fire and famine" syndrome — all weaken the poem to the point where it is little better than music hall melodrama. Technically too it has faults which the original poem lacked. It begins by using the decasyllabic line, much more flaccid than the compact octosyllabic line of the first poem. Line lengths vary throughout the poem giving it an un-planned, errant air as compared with the tight construction of the earlier verses. Kendall seems to have read and been impressed by the extended Homeric similes of Matthew Arnold's "Sohrab and Rustum." He constructs similar lengthy analogies:

> As fares a swimmer, who hath lost his breath
> In 'wildering seas afar from any help —
> Who, fronting Death, can never realize
> The dreadful Presence, but is prone to clutch
> At every weed upon the weltering wave;
> So fared the watcher, poring o'er the last
> Of him she loved, with dazed and stupid stare;
> Half-conscious of the sudden loss and lack
> Of all that bound her life, but yet without
> The power to take her mighty sorrow in.

It is a brave attempt but it is open to the same criticism levelled at Arnold's use of it. It impedes the simple movement of the poem and adds ornamentation where none is required. And Kendall's simile lacks, of course, the poetic quality and the precise pictorial clarity which characterized Arnold's analogies.

Three years later Kendall revived the "death in the bush" theme again. He removed the artificial opening and concluding lines (about 110 lines in all) with their weak device of cruel wrong and ultimate honour regained, then presented it under the pseudonym "Arakoon," as an entrant in *Williams's Illustrated Australian Annual* competition of 1868. The judge, R. H. Horne, praised it highly and awarded it the prize. In a letter to the poet, January 19, 1869, he spoke of the "great advances" Kendall's poetry had made since his first volume. If "A Death in the Bush," the 1868 variant of the original 1860 "A Death Scene in the Bush," is used as a yardstick, Horne's judgment did little service to Kendall's earlier poetry.

V *The Aborigines*

The aborigines were a further essential component of the "spirit of place" to which Kendall was so committed. Earlier colonial writers had displayed uncertainty in handling the aboriginal theme, ignoring the black man whenever possible or picturing him as the monstrous human equivalent of the other natural freaks of the antipodean world — oddities such as reversed seasons, flightless birds and bounding marsupials.

Kendall's poems on aboriginal themes in this first collection are "Kooroora, "Urara" and "Ulmarra." Both "Urara" and "Ulmarra" were printed in the *Clarence and Richmond Examiner* on April 15, 1862, under the general title "Aboriginal Death Songs." "Kooroora" which tells of the death of a warrior in battle, could also be included in that category. These early poems fix on legendary tribal battles with the traditional accompaniment of fallen warriors, grief-stricken maidens and desolate landscapes whose streams run red with blood. They also convey something of the romanticizing of primitives which was a phenomenon of world literature in the first half of the nineteenth century and represent Kendall's efforts to invest the aboriginal with some of the mystique of the "noble savage" which appears in American writers such as J. Fenimore Cooper and Longfellow.

"Kooroora"[25] tells of the warrior chief of the Wahibbi who is aroused from his dreams of ancient battles to face a real one. The Wanneroos are rampaging through the bush, thirsty for his blood.

> He starts from his sleep and he clutches his spear,
> And the echoes roll backward in wonder,
> For a shouting strikes into the hollow woods near,
> Like the sounds of a gathering thunder.

> He clambers the ridge with his face to the light,
> The foes of Wahibbi come full in his sight —
> The waters of Mooki will redden to-night.
> Go! and glory awaits thee Kooroora.

Kooroora falls before the onslaught and his bones are left to bleach in the forest. The eight-lined stanza, rhythmically attractive, creates an air of rising tension which builds up to a peak in the invocation of the final line. The final line in each stanza also provides a summary of the action to that point. Aboriginal battle implements such as the boomerang, spear and yeelaman, together with a sprinkling of gutturally musical aboriginal names,, "Wanneroo," "Wahibbi," "Kooroora," "Mooki" and "Ewalli" impart some slight air of authenticity to the poem.

"Urara"[26] is a lamentation for the warriors who have fallen that day. During a pause in the battle the tribe's survivors crouch in the cold ashes of the camp fires, their faces buried in their knees, and keen over those who have died. The dirgelike refrain at the end of each of the three verses, based on the gloomy name of the river itself, envelops the poem in that melodious but lugubrious air that Kendall loved so well:

> But the low winds sigh,
> And the dead leaves fly,
> Where our warriors lie,
> In the Dingoes den — in the white-cedar glen
> On the banks of the gloomy Urara!
> Urara! Urara!
> On the banks of the gloomy Urara!

"Ulmarra"[27] employs a similar refrain and an equally mournful assonance as it singles out one grieving maiden who ". . . sitteth there weeping/Weeping, and weeping, and weeping,/For the face of a warrior sleeping." Kendall's interest in the romanticized aboriginal theme reached its peak in the widely anthologized "The Last of His Tribe."[28] Published in the *Sydney Morning Herald* September 30, 1864, about two years after the poems just mentioned, it was included in *Leaves from Australian Forests*, Kendall's second volume. Its opening lines reveal an old warrior, the last gaunt survivor of his race:

> He crouches, and buries his face on his knees,
> And hides in the dark of his hair;

> For he cannot look up to the storm-smitten trees,
> Or think of the loneliness there:
> Of the loss and the loneliness there.

He dreams of the battles and the hunts of long ago, the corroboree "warlike and grim," the lubra who tended his fire and was mother of his children. The bush animals, when they become aware of his silent presence, scurry off in fear: "But he sits in the ashes and lets them pass/Where the boomerang sleeps with the spear:/With the nullah, the sling, and the spear." He looks now for death, then reunion with his tribe who have vanished with the years:

> Will he go in his sleep from these desolate lands,
> Like a chief, to the rest of his race,
> With the honey-voiced woman who beckons, and stands,
> And gleams like a Dream in his face —
> Like a marvellous Dream in his face?

The poem pictures the destruction of the aboriginal race but makes little or no attempt to blame the white man, attributing the aboriginal demise to the inevitable onward march of progress. The poem shows that as early as Kendall's day the decimation of the tribes was well advanced yet only occasionally did it emerge as a subject for sensitive Australians to deplore. Harpur's "An Aboriginal Mother's Lament" sympathized with the aboriginals. George Gordon McCrae's two aboriginal narratives, "Mamba the Bright-Eyed" and "Balladeadro" (both published in 1867), show his feelings aroused for the natives. Later poets such as Dame Mary Gilmore were much more accusatory. In her volume *The Wild Swan* she recreates the horror of the gunyah burned to ashes by the white settler, of the fear-crazed black men and women driven to their deaths in the swamps by his vicious dogs, of the lubra lamenting her slain child. She pictured the land itself disconsolate at the slaughter: "The Murrumbidgee whispering at its bank cries,/'Where are they/ Whose thousand campfires drove the darkness of the night away?'"

Fifteen years after "The Last of His Tribe" Kendall turned again to the subject of aboriginals. These later poems are devoid of poetic quality. They are tasteless skits, doggerel-type verses whose only purpose seemed to be to lampoon the unfortunate blacks who clung to the fringes of white society. They highlight, unintentionally perhaps, the moral and physical disintegration of those aboriginals who had lost the dignity of their own culture and who aped,

pathetically, the customs and mannerisms of the white man. The
grotesque monstrosities, "Black Lizzie," "Black Kate" and "Jack the
Blackfellow" are typical of the contemptuous and derisory, though
supposedly good-natured, mockery of the aboriginals so popular at
the time. The unlovely subject matter, the satirical tone, and the
strongly flavoured colloquial language (Kendall seldom used the
Australian vernacular in his serious works) make these among the
least attractive of Kendall's poems, as the following extracts show.

> Still if the charm called Beauty lies
> In ampleness of ear and lip,
> And nostrils of exceeding size,
> You are a gem, my ladyship.
>
> . . . .
>
> Your people — take them as a whole —
> Are careless on the score of grace;
> And hence you needn't comb your poll
> Or decorate your unctuous face.
>
> . . . .
>
> Still seeing that a little soap
> Would soften an excess of tint
> You'll pardon my advance, I hope
> In giving you a gentle hint."
>
> I never loved a nigger belle —
> My tastes are too aesthetic!
> The perfume from a gin is — well,
> A rather strong emetic.
>
> . . . .
>
> No gushing girl in Fancy's dream
> Perceives her "fairy prince" in you:
> You are, you beggar, what you seem —
> A fusty darkie through and through.
>
> And as to moral beauty, why —
> This ugly thief — he wouldn't pass
> His neighbour's leg of mutton by —
> Supposing it were worth a glass.
>
> *He* go to church! His Paradise,
> My simple friend, is yonder bar;
> There is no heaven in his eyes
> But where the grog and 'bacca' are.[29]

VI   *The Young Patriot*

Kendall was the son of a "Currency Lass" and he grew up, as did many others who were born in Australia, with a weaker attachment to the old world than those who had reluctantly broken homeland ties to come here. There was still much about life in the colony in midcentury to offend the sensitivities of those who remembered the gentler, more civilized society they had left behind in England. But after transportation of convicts ceased in the 1840s New South Wales gradually began to lose the character of a jail, the bawdy, rowdy, desperate, rum-ridden atmosphere giving way to a thriving, industrious commercialism. New arrivals in Sydney would have been reminded of England by the many elegant houses and commercial premises that reflected the beauty and charm of borrowed English architecture. Yet much was still strange and alien. Manners were rough and ready; there was a lack of regard for the conventions held dear back home; the streets were dusty; the heat intolerable; the bush close and menacing. For the older people affinity with the new land seemed impossible. But for their children, born here and growing up to accept these conditions as normal, there was a feeling of hopeful anticipation, a sense of pride in the possibilities that the country offered. Kendall was quick to express this emerging feeling of expectancy and promise. His early poem, "The Far Future,"[30] only the third that he had published, looks optimistically toward Australia's future place in the world. Published in the *Australian Home Companion and Band of Hope Journal*, November 5, 1859, when Kendall was only twenty-one, the poem bore the signature E. H. Kendall. It has been suggested, but not certainly established, that this signature implies join authorship by Henry and his twin brother, Basil Edward, or Edward, as he was known. The poem is remarkably direct, for those colonial times, in its condemnation of the old world — "the ruins and wrecks of the Past" — and in its brash prediction that the Australia of the future would outshine the glory of the mother country. Such presumption would have been offensive to English readers of the day. Kendall's gesture of apology to ruffled feelings appears in a footnote to the line "the yoke of dependence aside will she cast." He explained: "I hope the above will not be considered disloyal. It is but reasonable to imagine that Australia will in the far future become an independent nation — that imaginaton springing as it does from a native-born Australian's brain."

Bernard O'Dowd, who wrote in the early years of the twentieth century, is usually acknowledged as the standard-bearer of the nationalist-radicals, those who believed in the vision of a "Great Australia" founded on the principles of freedom and equality. His patriotic classic, *The Bush*, published in 1912, gives the Australia of the future a place of glory and grandeur in centuries yet to come similar to that held by the civilizations of Greece and Rome in the ancient world. A temple of "freedom and glory," her ideal society of the future will have eliminated all injustice and oppression. Kendall's "The Far Future" says the same thing — equally as effectively, much more succinctly and half a century earlier. It is one of his poetic achievements that has so far evaded recognition:

> Australia, advancing with rapid wing'd stride,
> Shall plant among nations her banner with pride,
> The yoke of dependence aside she will cast,
> And build on the ruins and wrecks of the Past.
> Her flag on the tempest will wave to proclaim
> 'Mong kingdoms and empires her national name.
> The future shall see it asleep or unfurl'd,
> The shelter of Freedom and boast of the world.
> Australia, advancing like Day on the sky,
> Has glimmered thro' darkness, will blazon on high,
> A Gem in its glitter has yet to be seen,
> When Progress has placed her where England has been;
> When bursting those limits above she will soar,
> Outstretching all rivals who've mounted before,
> And, resting will blaze with her glories unfurl'd,
> The empire of empires and boast of the world.

The jingoistic tones, inflated rhetoric, and sonorous phrases in glorification of national power are all characteristic of the patriotic poetry of the age and can be ignored. The significance of the poem is that in colonial times when deprecation of this antipodean world was both the social and literary fashion it attempts to create new loyalties toward the land with which the colonists' lives were now linked. It is additional evidence that throughout this first volume of poems Kendall was taking his "Native Australian Poet" tag very seriously.

CHAPTER 3

Kendall's Poetry:
The Middle Period

I   Leaves From Australian Forests

SEVEN years elapsed between Kendall's first volume, *Poems and Songs*, and his second collection, *Leaves from Australian Forests*. They were troubled years which brought him many personal problems. Although he was now well aware of public apathy towards Australian writers — he had only to remember Harpur — he had hoped to receive sympathetic and generous nurture of his own literary talents. When this did not eventuate as fully as he had expected he grew petulant, then bitter. He received genuine encouragement from some reviewers and critics and support from a small, influential group of literati including J. Sheridan Moore, J. L. Michael, N. D. Stenhouse, Dr. John Woolley, Edward Kennedy Silvester (poet and critic), Richard Rowe ("Peter Possum" of the *Sydney Morning Herald*) and William Wilkes, one of the first sketchers of Australian bush life. But, after the initial favorable response there was no sustained or widespread interest in his poetry. The unsold volumes of *Poems and Songs* languished until 1864 when Kendall withdrew them from sale.

For a variety of reasons — money troubles, family discord, failure to advance in his Civil Service career, fading friendships with Sydney people, hopes for greater success in Melbourne — he resigned from the New South Wales Civil Service and on April 1, 1869, an ironic choice of dates for beginning a new life, left for Victoria. There, six months later, in October, 1869, he published *Leaves from Australian Forests*.

This new volume was to meet much the same fate as the first. There were only 1500 copies printed, selling at five shillings each. After Kendall died, a dozen years later, there were still several hundred for sale in Melbourne at sixpence apiece. Alexander Sutherland,

58 HENRY KENDALL

who was the first to edit collections of Kendall's poetry after his
death, in attempting to explain the lack of interest in Kendall's second volume, pictures, without apology, the prevailing colonial attitudes to the local literary products:

And yet there are good and sufficient reasons why poetry should not be a
highly paid commodity here. The readers who are fond of poetry — perhaps
one in ten of general public — find to their hand a quantity of first-class
poetry which may well serve for the reading of a lifetime. Shakespeare,
Milton, Spenser, Byron, Wordsworth, Shelley — how many are there who
can say they have read the whole works of these authors? Perhaps one in five
hundred. But even to the reader who has become familiar with these, there
opens out numerous others not at all inferior to them — Burns, Cowper,
Tennyson, Longfellow, Keats, Coleridge, Campbell, Poe, Scott and a host of
poets whose complete works can generally be had for a few shillings; hence
the great bulk of the public have still abundance of first-rate poetry to
peruse, and never have occasion to resort to the second rate, which is all that
the colonies have as yet to show. . . . The Australian is decidedly an eclectic.
He reads the best he can get from England, Scotland, Ireland, or America,
with impartial mind; and as there are at least sixty poets in the English
language superior to Kendall, the ordinary reader is not likely to reach so far
down in the list ere his poetry-reading days come to an end.[1]

Despite its failure to sell readily there was a favorable critical reaction to *Leaves From Australian Forests.* In the *Colonial Monthly
Magazine* of October, 1869, George Oakley ("Evelyn") drew some
deft comparisons between Kendall and his fellow colonial, Charles
Harpur, objected mildly to Kendall's "curious alliterative
phraseology," and must have gratified Kendall's ego by judging him
"the first poet in whom, it may be said, Australia speaks."

The new collection contained forty-five poems and a group of
twelve sonnets. A further fifty-one poems, not included in the collection, can be traced to the period of seven years between the two
books. *Leaves from Australian Forests* was dedicated to Kendall's
young wife, Charlotte. In the short poem, "Dedication,"[2] he speaks
of his gratitude for her love and loyalty in their difficult first year
and a half of marriage. It is a touching tribute but in the light of the
domestic disasters that were to follow in the next few years
"Dedication's" apology for past neglect and its optimism for their
future ring rather hollow. An interesting feature of the poem is Kendall's disgruntled complaint about " . . . the life austere/That waits
upon the man of letters here," a complaint he was to repeat, in much

the same words in "Araluen," 1879, and in the memorial verses to
Marcus Clarke, 1881.

The real opening of the new volume is in the two "Prefatory
Sonnets"[3] which follow "Dedication." Kendall had been convinced,
both by his own instincts and by early Romantic nature philosophy
as articulated by Wordsworth, whom Harpur strongly commended
to him, that poetry ought to be securely rooted in the landscape
matrix and that nature offered the finest focus for the concentration
of poetry. The opening prefatory sonnet explains his original ambition to create pure, unspoiled nature poetry, in which there would
have been perfect harmony between the "words" (his poetry) and
the "music" and "colours" of nature:

> I purposed once to take my pen and write
> Not songs like some tormented and awry
> With Passion, but a cunning harmony
> Of words and music caught from glen and height,
> And lucid colours born of woodland light,
> And shining places where the sea-streams lie.

An obsession for language tailored to the precise demands of thought
(and similarly of description) is evident in his comment to Charles
Harpur, as early as September 25, 1862: "I think that there is a fear-
ful gap between thought and language. Perhaps there is no rarer endowment of the poet than the gift of *exact* expression — the power of
subjugating language to thought; so he can conscientiously feel that
the whole truth which was in him has been laid before the world in
all its unclouded simplicity."

By 1869, when the "Prefatory Sonnets" were written, he had
accepted that his original goal of "a cunning harmony" was a "faded
purpose" which he was unlikely to achieve. He was now prepared to
settle for "fruits" that were less than "faultless," for "certain
syllables" which lacked the once-desired perfection and precision
but which had some beauty nevertheless, because they were
borrowed ". . . from unfooted dells/And secret hollows dear to noontide dew." The regretful tone of the poem shows that he looked
upon his compromise as a diminished thing, yet the attainment of
the goal he had originally set himself — strikingly beautiful but
largely impersonal poetry — would have made him nothing more
than a technically accurate painter of the visual patterns of nature.
None of the poetic predecessors that he was drawn to would have

been satisfied with that achievement. The eighteenth-century poets, Gray, Collins, Cowper, Thomson; the early Romantics, Wordsworth and Coleridge; the American nature poets, William Cullen Bryant and Emerson, had all been, in varying degrees, deeply and personally involved — as interpreters of nature not simply descriptive artists. Like them, Kendall could never have remained so aloof as not to intrude something of his own "tormented and awry" passions into his songs. The "certain syllables" that he now proposed to borrow from the "unfooted dells" had to come, as they had always done in the past, as much from his own personality as from the landscape. It was his personality which created that highly subjective, emotional perspective which dominated his landscape poetry, preventing it from being dominated in turn by the inanimate, picturesque, visible shapes and forms of nature.

The second prefatory sonnet is a whimsical, clever apologia for his borrowings from contemporary English poets. On September 25, 1862, he had sought correspondence with Charles Harpur, hoping to gain "mentally" from the relationship. As he put it winningly, "we cannot leave a cedar grove without carrying away some of the fragrance." The echoes of the great writers in his own poetry are equally neatly explained by his comment in this sonnet: ". . . think how from its neighbouring, native sea/The pensive shell doth borrow melody." As if to illustrate his unrepentant attitude over the unforgivable crime (in the nineteenth century) of reflecting the language, ideas and techniques of more illustrious literary figures he concluded the sonnet with an amusing and extremely apt sestet which is strongly and ironically reminiscent of the finale of Arnold's "The Scholar Gipsy":

> Lo, when a stranger, in soft Syrian glooms
> Shot through with sunset, treads the cedar dells,
> And hears the breezy ring of elfin bells
> Far down by where the white-haired cataract booms,
> He, faint with sweetness caught from forest smells,
> Bears thence, unwitting, plunder of perfumes.

All three colonial poets, Harpur, Kendall and Gordon, were eager readers of the "new" English poets, although Harpur, a generation older than the other two, had more affinity with Wordsworth than with the later writers Tennyson, Browning, Arnold, Rossetti and Swinburne. These Victorian-era poets were not widely available;

given the inevitable colonial time lag in literary taste, they were then only barely known and dimly understood. The small colonial literary clique, however, which did keep abreast of literary fashions, tended to reflect these new writers. Kendall's knowledge and awareness of those nineteenth-century "avant-gardes" is apparent in his letters to Harpur:

Tennyson is over-rated and under-rated. One of the best lyrics in the language is "Locksley Hall" — one of the vilest poems in the same tongue is "Maud." The "Two Voices" will be more generally admitted as Tennyson's completest and most direct work yet. With him Art rules thought like an Autocrat. His most ardent admirers must admit that the "mechanism" of his Poetry delights him more than doth the Poetry itself. The trouble evidently expended over the excruciatingly elaborate "Idylls of the King" will bear witness so far. "In Memoriam" is one of the noblest things of its kind, that has been given to us this century. But I can't help suspecting that Tennyson will be chiefly remembered through passages, not through *poems in their completeness.*

Later the same year there is a reconsideration of Tennyson's *Idylls of the King.* "You may not have read the "Idylls of the King" — in which I think some of the most melodious blank verse in the English language is to be found. Milton's verse is like Beethoven's music, Shelley's like Mozart's, and Tennyson's like Handel's. The first *rolls,* the second *gushes,* and the third *flows."* In 1865 he wrote, "Tennyson's last volume [probably *Enoch Arden]* was comparatively a very poor affair. Not so that by Robert Browning [*Dramatis Personae].* It is a book of steel and gold. I hope you have heard of the new poet Algernon Charles Swinburne — a writer as luxuriant as Keats and as lyrical as Shelley."[4] His knowledge of these new literary figures, his capacity to analyze their attitudes and techniques, his incorporation of their styles and ideas into his own poetry, made him a rare phenomenon in the colonial literary scene. Yet Kendall was not merely an imitator of the mid-Victorians. His own poetic outlook was largely already formed and if the new writers struck responsive chords in him it was because those chords were already there. This literary coincidence has sometimes been deplored by Kendall's critics who believe that the verbal luxuriance, metrical slickness, sentimentality and subjectivity of these writers were the worst influences to which he could be exposed. Given the example of writers who employed, in Judith Wright's words, "a simpler, and stronger line, a practice of verbal economy, a study of poetic structure,"[5] these critics feel that Kendall would have been a different, and better, poet. Just as clearly the new and better poet would not have been Henry Kendall.

After the explanations made by the "Prefatory Sonnets" the nature of the poetry of this second volume begins to emerge. There are two main types of poetry — lyric and narrative. The lyrics are chiefly set against the background of the Australian landscape; the narratives have Australian themes and themes borrowed from the Bible and classical myth. The landscape poems established Kendall's reputation as Australia's chief nature poet but that reputation has been strongly challenged in recent years. The narratives have not, until recently, been considered seriously. It is ironic, but probably a matter of fact, that if Kendall's reputation as a major Australian poet is to be preserved in the future it will be the narratives as much as the lyrics that will be used on his behalf. In *Leaves from Australian Forests*, and in the contemporary uncollected poems, there is also an important section of love poetry and a number of "In Memoriam" poems that are worthy of comment.

II *Landscape Lyrics*

About a third of the poems in the 1869 volume are "landscape" lyrics, elaborate word-pictures which squander themselves in a flood of extravagant meaningless sound. Occasionally they are given some point by the poet's melancholy introspection. Such poems, vaguely representing the continuation of his desire to impregnate his poetry with the Australian "spirit of place," — first seen in *Poems and Songs* — include the well-known "Bell Birds," "September in Australia," "Araluen," "The Warrigal" and "Coogee."

Although "Bell Birds"[6] has become accepted as a "classic" Kendall poem it owes some of its character to notes supplied by Charles Harpur when he published his long poem "The Kangaroo Hunt or a Morning in the Bush" in the *Australian Home Companion and Band of Hope Journal* over several issues in 1859 - 60. Kendall's poem appeared years later in the *Sydney Morning Herald*, November 25, 1867. Harpur's notes read:

The channels or water-courses of summer-shrunk lagoons are called *blind* creeks. The term, I believe, is of colonial growth, and very appropriate; those channels being ... matted over with sedge and other water grasses. ... This remarkable little bird — the bell-bird — is chiefly to be found in such mountain ravines as reserve a constant supply of water — its

note being an infallible assurance of the vicinity of that element; that it is lying in the rock-tanks somewhere at hand, however hiddenly or noiselessly sliding through some concealed cleft. Hence though the tone of its note is 'pensive' in seeming, it is exceedingly grateful to the thirsty wayfarer. Each bird emits but a single sound, like the tinkle of a very small bell; but when there are many of them in the vicinity, as there mostly are, disposed at equal distances in the surrounding trees, an irregular chime 'most unusual, most melancholy', is kept ringing about one with an effect that is very wild and singular, and though always by association lonesome, yet pleasing in the extreme.[7]

Harpur's "channels," "matted . . . with sedge," "the thirsty wayfarer," and "irregular chime" which keeps "ringing about one," are transferred more or less directly into Kendall's poem. Such borrowing of phrases from these notes does not mean that Kendall is merely describing, in his poem, a piece of Harpur landscape. Bellbirds were plentiful in the rain forest escarpments of the South Coast where Kendall had grown up; he needed no prompting from Harpur to picture their favorite haunts.

"Bell Birds" exists on two levels. If one surrenders to the flood of musical sounds and pictorial phrases without worrying about meaning or sense then the poem is a heady experience. There is some justification for reacting to it in just that way. Many readers have done so. But "Bell Birds" is so technically flawed that despite its considerable superficial attractiveness the faults greatly diminish it. It begins with an expressive picture of the bellbird's cool, moist haunts: "By channels of coolness the echoes are calling,/And down the dim gorges I hear the creek falling." But the clear direction that the poem seems to be taking from the opening couplet is immediately abandoned. The succeeding three couplets are vague and confused. The second, "It lives in the mountain where moss and the sedges/Touch with their beauty the banks and the ledges" is quite indefinite. Is "it" the creek or the bellbird? If the bellbird, why the use of the singular since the other references in the poem are plural? If the creek, why prolong the reference to it and why limit its locale to the mountains? The third couplet, "Through breaks of the cedar and sycamore bowers/Struggles the light that is love to the flowers" adds a further central figure "the light" — where before there was the bellbird and/or the creek — and an irrelevant reference to "flowers." The final couplet, "And, softer than slumber and sweeter than singing,/The notes of the bell-birds are running and ringing"

brings in the first direct reference to the bellbirds and then only to their song. It also contains two inept analogies — comparing the bird's song to slumber and to singing. The bellbird's note is a distinctive metallic chime — neither soft nor sweet. Of what descriptive value is the phrase "softer than slumber?" How soft is slumber? If it were "softer than slumber," whatever that is, would it be audible at all? The analogy is nonsense and the phrase itself is only a trite, poetic figure. "Sweeter than singing" is equally poor. The repeated chiming note of many bellbirds, one after the other (in essence, their song anyway), is an unusual sound experience, but as the many Australians who have heard it will agree, it has no quality of sweetness at all. The couplet has no descriptive relevance to its subject, the phrases being chosen purely because Kendall saw them as poetically picturesque.

The third stanza moves away from the bellbirds to describe the impact of spring on the cool mountain fastnesses, the month of October being personified in a stereotyped, traditional manner. The lines are filled with languid, ornate phrases, heavy with alliteration that rolls sweetly, and meaninglessly, off the tongue in the true Kendall fashion:

> October, the maiden of bright yellow tresses,
> Loiters for love in these cool wildernesses;
> Loiters, knee deep, in the grasses, to listen,
> Where dripping rocks gleam and the leafy pools glisten:
> Then is the time when the water-moons splendid
> Break with their gold, and are scattered or blended
> Over the creeks, till the woodlands have warning
> Of songs of the bell-bird and wings of the Morning.

The rising tide of alliteration runs unchecked through the next stanza reaching its peak in the almost tongue twisting final couplet: "With ring and with ripple, like runnels whose torrents/Are toned by the pebbles and leaves in the currents." The final stanza, in which Kendall projects himself into his bellbird landscape, brings some significance into this orgy of sound and colour. In the wistful, melancholy throb of the final lines lies the appeal that has beguiled so many sentimental readers. Kendall, like Wordsworth, gains much from his recollections of natural beauty. Wordsworth, "in lonely rooms" amid "the din of towns and cities," owed to the beauty of the Wye valley many later moments of "tranquil restoration." Kendall is similarly indebted to his bellbird landscape:

Often I sit, looking back to a childhood,
Mixt with the sights and the sounds of the wildwood,
Longing for power and the sweetness to fashion,
Lyrics with beats like the heart-beats of Passion; —
Songs interwoven of lights and of laughters
Borrowed from bell-birds in far forest-rafters;
So I might keep in the city and alleys
The beauty and strength of the deep mountain valleys;
Charming to slumber the pain of my losses
With glimpses of creeks and a vision of mosses.

This is the best stanza, really the only good one, in the poem. There is the familiar Kendall desire — to create poetry as beautiful as the landscape which inspires it, as moving as the strongest human emotions. Such poetry, could he fashion it, would bring delight in the dreary years that Kendall believes all human beings inevitably come to know.

Such criticism of Kendall's popular lyric is purely destructive, and it is doubtful whether even the greatest poetry is proof against a rigorous and carping examination of its every phrase. But "Bell Birds" calls for such close scrutiny because it is the typical Kendall lyric, providing one of the clearest examples of his surrender to the hypnotic effect of a rich flow of sensuous sound which, in the end, destroys the sense and meaning of the poem. There are critics who defend "Bell Birds" against the kind of charges made here. They believe that Kendall's imprecision is deliberate, that he blends all the elements of his poem — the birds and their music, the cool glades, his own memories — into an organic but deliberately inchoate whole. He is trying to create

a private sanctuary out of time, remote from the tyranny of the city and its alleys, and safe from the oppression of the sun and heat. We penetrate beyond the temporal and mutable to a timeless and changeless existence. It is both real and unreal — unreal, because we can't really know it, except from such fragmentary evidence as the bell-birds, the creeks, the echoes and the dazzling lyre-bird, and yet real precisely because we have that evidence. The bell-birds exist only as voices and songs, they are not seen.[8]

Viewed in this way the poem becomes a type of literary mood painting, a blurred, vague reverie in which the poet's mind, freed from the demands of syntax and logical arrangement, luxuriates in an abandoned fusion and confusion of sense impressions — "childhood" and "wildwood," sunshine and showers, bird songs and

poet songs. Something of this quality the poem does have. But it is not the product of deliberate, skilled artistry; it is the accidental but inevitable result of the poet's inability to withstand the temptation and excitement of stringing together phrase after facile phrase.

There is no indication that Kendall thought very highly of the poem. He seems to have made only one reference to it and that was briefly in a letter to P. J. Holdsworth from Gosford, October 13, 1874. Holdsworth had sent him a poem "The Valley of the Popran" which contained some description of bellbirds. Kendall wrote:

"The Valley of the Popran" is the most exquisite lyric you have written. Nothing could be finer than the bit about the bell-birds. . . . [I do not] care for the application of the word 'grand' to the hymns of the bell-birds. . . . Bell-birds by the way never take to blackbutt trees — the blackbutt being a native of the open forest land . . . you can get things right by bringing in some brush tree — the cedar — the blue gum — baglan — wild hazel — or wattle for example. I believe in all you say about the bell-bird. Nothing can be more delicious than

> "Yellow-bosomed bell-birds smite
> Crisp air with clarions of delight."
> You may remember that I once wrote of them myself.

"September in Australia,"[9] an equally popular Kendall landscape lyric, is flawed in much the same way as "Bell Birds" — clarity and meaning being sacrificed for word music. The opening lines, though full of poetic clichés, have a sense of purpose and direction:

> Grey winter hath gone, like a wearisome guest
> And, behold, for repayment,
> September comes in with the wind of the West
> And the Spring in her raiment!

Then, as in "Bell Birds," the direction and purpose are obscured by picturesque, but empty, description. An outburst of musical mumbo jumbo, which presumably describes the magic of Spring's arrival, follows:

> The ways of the frost have been filled of the flowers
> While the forest discovers
> Wild wings with the halo of hyaline hours,
> And a music of lovers.

The reader, puzzling over the meaning of the line "wild wings with the halo of hyaline hours," is given little time for reflection, but is hurried on by a flow of mesmerizing, musical phrases into further obscurities. The stream, from its source "in the hollow hill" slips along "in a darling old fashion" — whatever kind of movement that might be. The fourth stanza attempts a philosophical relationship between nature and human life, but nothing is enunciated clearly or meaningfully:

> The West, when it blows at the fall of the noon,
> And beats on the beaches,
> Is filled with a tender and tremulous tune
> That touches and teaches:
> The stories of Youth, of the Burden of Time,
> And the death of Devotion,
> Come back with the wind, and are themes of the rhyme,
> In the waves of the ocean.

What is "the fall of the noon"? Should it be "moon"? Does the "tender and tremulous tune" of the West wind carry the story of life? Is life's story a composite of the "stories of Youth," the "burden of Time" and the "death of Devotion"? Is life's story also the "themes of the rhyme," that is, the themes of his poem? What is the connection between the "rhyme" and "the waves of the ocean"? There is a general vague drift of meaning which may satisfy the "mood painting" reader but the lines defy logical analysis.

The next verse brings Kendall into his landscape. Only then does the poem become properly meaningful. He shares with the spring maiden "September" his thoughts of another maiden, who has been taken from him. One is reminded of the lost maiden of his earlier "Aidenn" poems:

> We, having a secret to others unknown,
> In the cool mountain-mosses,
> May whisper together, September, alone
> Of our loves and our losses.

The following two verses picture the turbulent nature of the Australian spring. The "hyaline" hours give way to gales and storms. Personification and metaphor run rampant. There is "the forehead of Morning" and "the steps of the Night" which are "heavy with warning." "Her voice" (but whose voice?) is "lofty and loud." She has hidden her eyes" in the clouds and "her feet in the surges"! The gale is "like a ghost." It moans in "the middle watch" and goes gliding "over and under" — over and under *what* is not revealed. The poem ends with the recognition that the music of spring is superior to the poet's own music; this serves, thankfully, as a reason for ending the poem — "its burden is ended." The final observation, trite and inevitably Romantic, is that the songs of spring will remain joyous to man forever. There is no better summary of this Kendall lyric than the judgment of another Australian poet, Kenneth Slessor, who said of it, "I can find little else except a confusion of high-sounding doubletalk that is made to seem more impressive by mechanical tricks."[10] The long-held critical opinion that Kendall's poetic strength lay in his lyric talent is scarcely substantiated by "Bell Birds" and "September in Australia," two of the most widely accepted samples of his lyric art.

In "Araluen" (the river poem)[11] he is less concerned with painting rich scenes of natural beauty. Instead he is involved more directly with human relationships, and true to his melancholy view of life, they are broken or lost relationships. On this occasion the lost one is a male friend. He is not necessarily a real person; he is described as "faithful friend beyond the main" and "friend of mine beyond the sea," commonplace figures in colonial literature which often spoke in melancholy terms of the separation from friends and loved ones back in England. Such a separation was not Kendall's own experience and he seems simply to have been exploiting this typical colonial situation. Remembering, however, that Kendall's paradise of "Aidenn" lay "beyond the sea" leads one to feel that the references in this poem may be figurative rather than literal. "Araluen" was published late in 1869 and James Lionel Michael, at one time Kendall's closest friend, and Charles Harpur, with whom he had such a strong affinity, had both died only the previous year. The references in the poem could then apply to either of those absent friends.

> Solace do I sometimes find
> Where you used to hear with me
> Songs of stream and forest-wind,
> Tones of wave and harp-like tree.
> . . . .
>
> Evermore in quiet lands,
> Friend of mine beyond the sea,

> Memory comes with cunning hands,
> Stays, and paints your face for me.

The landscape images of the poem are mainly water images. Kendall
was obsessed with moving water — rivers, creeks, mountain springs,
waterfalls, ocean waves. Such images find their best expression in
later "river" poems, "Mooni" "Narrara Creek" and "Orara," but
they are also in evidence here. Araluen is a

> River, myrtle-rimmed, and set
> Deep amongst unfooted dells —
> Daughter of grey hills of wet,
> Born by mossed and yellow wells.

As in "Bell Birds" there is emphasis on the restorative effect of
bushland beauty on the human spirit:

> Cities soil the life with rust:
> Water-banks are cool and sweet:
> River, tired of noise and dust
> Here I come to rest my feet.

The banal last line is disappointing but the simple "waterbanks are
cool and sweet" is more evocative than the effusions of the other two
poems. Kendall endowed the adjective "cool," which he loved to
use, with intimate and sensuous overtones. In the enervating heat
and humidity of the coastal Australian summer the body craves the
coolness of tree-shaded waters. Sensual gratification is conveyed in
the way Kendall lengthens and emphasizes the sound of the word,
almost caressing it as he uses it. In the other landscape images he
lapses into his usual faults — trite or tortured imagery in "blue-eyed
days" and "leaves of shine"; overworked personification in
"Summer's large luxurious eyes" and Winter's "eyes of ruth";
sacrifice of meaning for sound in "the month from shade to
sun/Fleets and sings supremest songs"; empty ornateness in
"cushioned tufts and turns/Where the sumptuous noontide lies";
and the inevitable flood of alliterative phrases such as "sings
supremest songs", "wilful woodwinds" and "pallid perished days."
  The attraction of "Araluen" is, as usual with this type of Kendall
poem, not so much the description of the landscape as the conjunction
of his emotions and the landscape, the setting of his own emotional
states into the landscape framework.

"The Warrigal,"[12] a popular "school-room" piece, describes the habitat of the dingo, the Australian native dog. It is a solitary world where the settler seldom ventured:

> The Warrigal's lair is pent in bare
> Black rocks at the gorge's mouth:
> It is set in ways where Summer strays
> Wth the sprites of flame and drouth;

The word "warrigal" was a somewhat poetic expression, the term "dingo" being more commonly used and certainly more suggestive of the "fierce and fickle and strange" nature of the animal it described. The poem's landscape is a mixture of derivative English expressions and local Australian phrases. Kendall speaks of "forest boles" instead of the more Australian "tree trunks," "marsh" and "fen" instead of "swamps," "fells" instead of "hills," "runnels" instead of "creeks," "glen" instead of "valley" and "hoarfrost" instead of "frost." It is difficult to know whether these English words were common in everyday speech in colonial times or whether Kendall used them merely as part of the stock "poetic" vocabulary. He also used Australian terms such as "gully," "gums," "waterholes," and "blind creeks," and these give the poem, in parts at least, an Australian flavor. He describes, from his memory of shepherding days, the nightly skulking of the dingo:

> In the gully-deeps, the blind creek sleeps;
> And the silver, showery, moon,
> Glides over the hills, and floats, and fills,
> And dreams in the dark lagoon;
> While halting hard by the station yard,
> Aghast at the hut-flame nigh,
> The Warrigal yells, and the flats and fells
> Are loud with his dismal cry.

> And strong streams flow, and great mists go,
> Where the Warrigal starts to hear
> The watch dog's bark break sharp in the dark,
> And flees like a phantom of Fear!

"The Warrigal" is a further example of Kendall's habit of injecting his own emotional tones into his landscapes. The setting is much the same as in "Bell Birds" and "September in Australia," but seen now as a backdrop to the menacing dingo, the shepherd's enemy, it is given overtones of gloom and threat. The description works toward conveying the sense of menace. Through the "bleak" mountains the "stormwind rolls"; the south wind "sobs" through "the moaning pines"; the "wild gums whistle and wail". The "sad marsh-fowl" and "the lonely owl" call dismally through "the fog-wreaths grey." Kendall maintains the flow of musical sound by his usual device of alliteration ("floats and fills," "flats and fells," "rippling runnel," "wild gums whistle and wail") augmented on this occasion by internal rhyme in each alternate line. The repetitive rhyme, allied to the metrical combination of iambics and anapests, produces a tripping, lilting movement which in the best lines beats out an attractive rhythm and at other times gives merely an exaggerated singsong effect.

Although in modern times "dingo" is a slang term to indicate cowardice, the poem carries a grudging note of admiration for the dog. The settlers certainly did not appreciate its depredations on their flocks and they needed all their skill and resources to cope with the animal. But its nature was not unlike their own. To survive constant privations and perils both animal and man had to possess resourcefulness, determination and even cunning. The final stanza tells of the dingo's share of these qualities:

> He roves through the lands of sultry sands,
> He hunts in the iron range,
> Untamed as surge of the far sea verge,
> And fierce and fickle and strange,
> The white man's track and the haunts of the black
> He shuns, and shudders to see;
> For his joy he tastes in lonely wastes
> Where his mate are torrent and tree.

In the final example of Kendall landscape lyric, "Coogee,"[13] the landscape first merges with and is then obliterated by the poet's melancholy. From its distinctive title — the name of a well-known Australian beach — the reader might expect to find recognizable physical characteristics, something to distinguish the setting as that one particular, individual stretch of the Pacific shoreline. But the poem has only a dim background of crags, breakers and sand, nothing more than a stereotyped poetic seascape that could have come from anywhere. Similar criticisms can be made of the landscapes of "Bell Birds," "September in Australia," "Araluen," and "The Warrigal." The succession of "dim gorges," "cool wildernesses," "echoing gorges," "valleys of coolness," "leafy pools," and "lonely wastes" provides unemphatic, indistinct, generalized pictures. To fellow poet J. Brunton Stephens, Kendall wrote "I am saturated with the peculiar spirit of Australian scenery, and, in painting that scenery, perhaps I excel."[14] These landscape poems fail to substantiate his claim, yet, for generations, Australian readers have been beguiled into mistaking the intention for the deed, been persuaded into accepting the vague images of the landscape lyrics as particularized Australian description. His generalized repetitive images convey almost nothing of the "peculiar spirit" of which Kendall spoke.

In "Coogee" the painting of the "peculiar spirit" of Australian scenery extends no further than the title itself. The poem begins promisingly, the opening line offering a focal point for detailed description, but, as in all these lyrics, the clarity of direction is not maintained. The succeeding lines describe only the vaguest, most generalized scene:

Sing the song of wave-worn Coogee — Coogee in the distance white
With its jags and points disrupted, gaps and fractures fringed with light!
Haunt of gledes and restless plovers of the melancholy wail
Ever lending deeper pathos to the melancholy gale.
There, my brothers, down the fissures, chasms deep and wan and wild,
Grows the sea-bloom, one that blushes like a shrinking fair blind child;
And amongst the oozing forelands many a glad green rock-vine runs,
Getting ease on earthy ledges sheltered from December suns.

In fairness to Kendall, even examining these lines apart from their supposed identification with a particular Australian beach scene brings little critical joy. The "jags and points disrupted" and the "gaps and fractures fringed with light" are meant to convey the rugged, saw-toothed effect of wind and sea-eroded rocks and cliffs but the lines fail to make definitive descriptive impact. Further on in the poem the gale is "melancholy," the plovers "restless," the pathos "deeper" — all tired worn-out images. The comparison of the sea-bloom to a "shrinking fair blind child" is aesthetically distasteful and rhythmically uncomfortable. The "glad green rock-vine runs" is a further sample of his taste for tongue-twisting, alliterative effects.

After the third stanza the landscape gives way to the customary preoccupation with melancholy thoughts — sad memories of the past; absent loved ones; and the once-fresh hopes of life, now withered. The "perished days" with their "sweet dead faces" haunt his memory. They are vanished days of youth which the sight of the gleaming beach revives in him, setting him "stumbling through dim summers once on fire" with love, friendship and hope. The present life is not unpleasant but it, and the future, can hold no glories to equal those of the past. On this note of gloomy nostalgia the poem ends:

Not that seasons bring no solace — not that time lacks lights and rest;
But the old things were the dearest, and the old loves seem the best.
We that start at songs familiar — we that tremble at a tone,
Floating down the ways of music, like a sigh of sweetness flown,
We can never feel the freshness — never find again the mood
Left amongst fair-featured places brightened of our brotherhood;
This, and this, we have to think of, when the night is over all,
And the woods begin to perish, and the rains begin to fall.

Although it is valid to criticise "Coogee," and other lyrics, for their technical faults it is unreasonable to attack them for the malaise of spirit that permeates them, or to attribute their faults to the Kendall gloom. Their faults are due to Kendall's lack of poetic, not personal, balance. To assert that he wrote badly in these lyrics because he was always emotionally out-of-sorts betrays a lack of familiarity with the poems themselves. Swinburne believed that it was the poet's genius ". . . to make sorrow sing/And mourning far more sweet than banqueting." Matthew Arnold was another contemporary whose poetic inclination was elegiac. Neither Swinburne nor Arnold is derided for his attitudes and it is wrong, and futile, to take Kendall to task for his sickly view of life. His morbidity was inherent, a physical and psychical predisposition over which he had little control. To blame him for his pessimistic and melancholy cast of mind is as senseless as blaming the dwarf for his diminished size. Hopkins spoke of the futility of such attitudes when he was enduring his own "dark night of the soul."

O the mind, mind has mountains; clifts of fall
Frightful, sheer, no-man-fathomed. Hold them cheap
May who ne'er hung there.

And, of course, for many readers the sad, melancholy air that clings to Kendall's lyrics has its own especial charm. It touches the ache of regret that exists in all of us, the same ache that Matthew Arnold's "Dover Beach" and Robert Frost's "The Road Not Taken" awaken so surely.

Kendall set his wistful, yearning self in the forefront of his landscapes; and suffused with the emotional glow from the poet, these landscapes have been the well-loved terrain of many Australians. A Kendall landscape poem without the Kendall emotions would be, to his devotees, as lacklustre as the churchyard at Stokes Poges without Gray's meditations or Tintern Abbey without Wordsworth's "sensations sweet." Araluen attracts because it is "Araluen! home of dreams!" not just a "River, myrtle-rimmed, and set/Deep amongst unfooted dells." September in Australia has her own springtime magic but her real glory is that she awakens nostalgic delights. Wth her the poet (and the reader), "May whisper together, September, alone,/Of our loves and our losses." The bellbirds bring to mind the beauty of cool mountain valleys but far more important is the flood of poignant life echoes that come with the memory of their chiming notes; echoes of all that is lost — youth, beauty, love itself. Judith Wright attributes the widespread appeal of these landscape lyrics to the fact that we can all recognize and share in their sentiments, that in fact "the foreground figure is not only Kendall, but humanity."[15]

III   Narrative Poems: Biblical and Classical

Kendall chose subjects for his narrative poems from the Old Testament and Greek mythology, and from local Australian events. Fifteen of Kendall's poems have biblical or classical subjects. They belong, mainly, to the years 1864 - 70, the second of Kendall's poetic periods. Nine of them were included in Leaves from Australian Forests and the remaining six, although published in newspapers and journals during that time, were discarded by Kendall in collating his second volume. Two of the rejected poems are entitled "Elijah" and another two, "Rizpah." Both these pairs of poems link biblical events to the contemporary scene in a rather clumsy, sermonizing manner. The "Elijah"[16] poems call for a present-day version of the old prophet, a "mighty spirit clad in shining arms of Truth," whose voice will descend "like thunder" on "our modern apathy." The "Rizpah"[17] poems compare the grief of Saul's concubine, whose sons were sacrificed to expiate the slaughter of the Gibeonites by Saul, with the sorrow of modern women, such as the American mothers who lost their sons in the Civil War. Two of the shorter poems in Leaves from Australian Forests are the companion

pieces "Daphne" and "Syrinx"[18] from Greek mythology. Kendall's
fancy was taken by the stories of the two Arcadian maidens, who
were saved from the pursuing deities Apollo and Pan, by being
transformed into the laurel tree (Daphne) and the river reed (Syrinx).
The twin poems, though slight, are winsome, amusing reenactments
of the lustful gods' futile chase.

The four main poems in this group are lengthy narratives and
deserve separate attention. They are "King Saul at Gilboa," "The
Voyage of Telegonus," "Ogyges" (all three published in *Leaves*)
and "Manasseh," which appeared in the *Australian Journal* in June,
1870, a few months after *Leaves* was published. Critical assessment
of these narratives down the years has been inconsistent and in-
conclusive. They have often been ignored completely. Sometimes
they have been dismissed as routine poetic exercises, something that
all poets come to attempt and few succeed in doing well. A typical
contemporary comment was Alexander Sutherland's observation in
1882 — "We cannot be supposed to hail these threadbare themes as
novelties . . . . 'Telegonus,' 'Ogyges,' 'Syrinx' and others are not
peculiarly suited for treatment by the Australian muse."[19] Archbishop Reed misses the value and significance of these poems, dismissing them without analysis.[20] Judith Wright fails to examine
them closely in her several discussions on Kendall, claiming that in
his treatment of biblical subjects the "shallowness of his feeling
reveals his lack of interest" and again that his biblical poems are
"colourless and unfelt."[21] It is hard to reconcile such comments with
Kendall's obvious pre-occupation with these themes and his inclusion of so many of these poems in his second volume.

T. Inglis Moore in his *Selected Poems of Henry Kendall*, 1957, was,
one of the first to suggest the quality of the narrative poems.

In his poems on classical themes or those on biblical subjects in a neo-
classical mode he can achieve the classic virtues: simplicity, clarity, detach-
ment and the force of economy. Thus "The Voyage of Telegonus" and
"King Saul at Gilboa," like such tales of the bush as "The Glen of Arrawatta"
and "A Death in the Bush" have true narrative, descriptive and dramatic
power. In such poems Kendall is stronger because he has passed beyond the
enervating pathos of his personal tragedy to an impersonal vigor.[22]

In their collaborative work on Kendall in the *Three Colonial Poets*
series, published in 1973, Kramer and Hope singled out the classical
and biblical narratives, especially "King Saul at Gilboa," for com-
mendation:

[It] is perhaps Kendall's most astonishing performance. . . . What is astonishing about the poem is the tragic force of its language and the tense driving energy of its verse. In spite of a few Victorian touches of language, it is essentially eighteenth-century verse and the models are Pope's *Homer* and Dryden's *Virgil*, particularly the latter. But it is by no means mere imitation of the heroic Augustan metres. It has an accent that is Kendall's own and shows that the Augustan style was still alive and developing in Australia in the 1860's. . . . It is a masterly performance in which the precipitous movement of the syntax reinforces the fatality and drama of the battle, while the stiffness of the verse form accentuates the impression of Saul's agony. In tragic force it would be hard to match in nineteenth-century English poetry, just as it would be hard to parallel the way in which a nineteenth-century poet is able to draw a new music from the Augustan instrument.

Their final judgment was: "Had Kendall always written like this he might be among the masters."[23]

IV   *"King Saul at Gilboa"*

The story of Saul, the first king of Israel, is one that would have had a natural appeal to Kendall. Saul was one of the Old Testament's most tempestuous figures, star-crossed, unlucky, a victim of his own indiscretions and impulsiveness. He was appointed King against the prophet Samuel's better judgment on the urging of the Israelites who cried "Appoint for us a King to govern us like all the nations." Time and again Saul saved Israel from its enemies, especially its traditional foes, the Philistines, but he came eventually to lose the approval of Samuel and the Lord. He took upon himself at Mizpah the priestly duties of making the burnt offering before the battle and, contrary to the Lord's command, spared the Amalekite herds after he had defeated Agag and the Amalekite people. As a punishment for his intractability "the Spirit of the Lord departed from Saul and an evil spirit from the Lord tormented Him." Retribution came in the final battle with the Philistines, the battle at Gilboa.

Kendall's poem[24] was first published in the *Empire* on New Year's Day 1869, and repeated at the end of January in the *Australasian*. The poem, in heroic couplets, opens with powerful driving meters that rise to a peak in the middle of the lines, then fall and rise again at the ends, conveying the sense of the ebb and flow of battle: quick spurts of violent activity followed by brief recuperative pauses:

> But swift and sure the spears of Ekron flew,
> Till peak and slope were drenched with bloody dew!

> "Shout, Timnath, shout!" the blazing leaders cried,
> And hurled the stone, and dashed the stave aside:
> "Shout, Timnath, shout! Let Hazor hold the height,
> Bend the long bow and break the lords of fight!"
> From every hand the swarthy strangers sprang,
> Chief leaped on chief, with buckler buckler rang!

Saul, with his army commander, Abner, is opposed by the Philistine chiefs, who take their names in the Old Testament fashion from the Philistine cities, Gaza, Gath and Ekron. The battle at first seems indecisive, but Saul's is a lost cause. Appalled by the might of the Philistines he had sought unsuccessfully, through omen and from the prophets, some indications of his chances of victory. Seeking other clairvoyant aid he had the witch of Endor contact the spirit of the dead prophet, Samuel. Samuel confirmed that the Lord was about to exact vengeance for Saul's disobedience in the affair of the Amalekites. He prophesied, "The Lord will give Israel also with you into the hands of the Philistines; and tomorrow, you and your sons shall be with me." Kendall's account of these events, slightly changed from the book of Samuel, tells crisply of the soothsayer's forecast of the battle:

> . . . he that fasted in the secret cave,
> And called up Samuel from the quiet grave,
> And stood with darkness and the mantled ghosts
> A bitter night on shrill Samarian coasts,
> Knew well the end: of how the futile sword
> Of Israel would be broken by the Lord;
> How Gath would triumph with the tawny line
> That bend the knee at Dagon's brittle shrine;
> And how the race of Kish would fall to wreck
> Because of vengeance stayed at Amalek.

The battle gradually turns against Israel. His sons slain, his commander in flight, the wounded, cornered King becomes the centre of Kendall's narrative. He is pursued by the Philistines' chosen marksmen, ten archers, especially charged with slaying him. Saul chooses suicide. Kendall employs the ironic variation which is in the second book of Samuel; an Amalekite slave rather than his armor bearer becomes the agent of suicide. In Saul's desperate commands to the Amakelite to do his bidding, the slave's repugnance and terror, his sudden impulsive moment of decision, there are obvious signs that Kendall was influenced by Tennyson's famous incident involving King Arthur, Sir Bedivere and the sword Excalibur. The similarity between the two scenes is reflected in the emotional attitudes and in the language:

> . . . At this the front of Saul
> Grew darker than a blasted tower wall;
> and seeing how there crouched upon his right
> Aghast with fear a black Amalekite
> He called and said, "I pray thee, man of pain,
> Red from the scourge, and recent from the chain,
> Set thou thy face to mine and stoutly stand
> With yonder bloody sword-hilt in thine hand
> And fall upon me." But the faltering hind
> Stood trembling like a willow in the wind.
> Then further, Saul: "Lest Ashdod's vaunting hosts
> Should bear me captive to their bleak-blown coasts,
> I pray thee, smite me: seeing peace has fled,
> And rest lies wholly with the quiet dead."
> At this a flood of sunset broke, and smote
> Keen blazing sapphires round a kingly throat
> Touched arm and shoulder, glittered in the crest,
> And made swift starlights on a jewelled breast!
> So, starting forward like a loosened hound,
> The stranger clutched the sword and wheeled it round,
> And struck the Lord's Anointed!

This reproduction of the scene from "The Passing of Arthur" was injudicious and Kendall has been roundly criticised for it. The lines which follow, more typically his own, describe the precipitate rush of the elated Philistine forces across the face of rugged Gilboa until their abrupt, awed halt before the dead Israelite king:

> . . . Fierce and fleet,
> Philistia came with shouts and clattering feet;
> By gaping gorges and by rough defile,
> Dark Ashdod beat across a dusty mile;
> Hot Hazur's bowmen toiled from spire to spire;
> And Gath sprang upwards like a gust of fire!
> On either side did Libnah's lords appear:
> And brass-clad Timnath thundered in the rear!
> "Mark, Achish, mark!" — South-west and south there sped
> A dabbled hireling from the dreadful dead!
> "Mark, Achish, mark!" — The mighty front of Saul,

> Great in his life and god-like in his fall!
> This was the arm that broke Philistia's pride
> Where Kishon chafes his seaward-going tide!
> This was the sword that smote till set of sun
> Red Gath from Michmash unto Ajalon!
> Low in the dust. And Israel scattered far!
> And dead the trumps, and crushed the hoofs of war!

The poem concludes with an emotional description of the battle's aftermath and the anguish of the defeated Israelites. The men of Jabesh-gilead recover the defiled body of Saul from its ignominious exhibition on the walls of Beth-shan and carry it secretly "athwart the place of tombs" (an exact phrase from Tennyson) to Jabesh where it is given proper ceremonial rites.

In choosing the tragic battle at Gilboa and Saul's death Kendall satisfies the classic requirements that the themes of great narrative poetry should be excellent human actions, actions which "most powerfully appeal to the great primary human affections." Matthew Arnold, in his influential *Preface* of 1853, had declared his belief that "a great human action of a thousand years ago is more interesting . . . than a smaller human action of today." Saul's death at Gilboa fulfills the Arnold ideal of a great action, noble personages, an intense situation. In the *Preface* Arnold had praised the ancients for their poetical theory:

With them the poetical character of the action in itself, and the conduct of it, was the first consideration; with us, attention is fixed mainly on the value of the separate thoughts and images which occur in the treatment of an action . . . with them the action predominated over the expression of it; with us, the expression predominates over the action. Not that they failed in expression, or were inattentive to it; on the contrary, they are the highest models of expression . . . but their expression is so excellent because it is so admirably kept in its right degree of prominence; because it is so simple and so well-subordinated; because it draws its force directly from the pregnancy of the matter which it conveys.[25]

Whether Kendall knew of Arnold's comments is difficult to ascertain. There is no reference to Arnold in Kendall's correspondence or in the prose articles on contemporary poets which Kendall wrote, mainly in the *Freeman's Journal* in 1871. Yet the links between the two are numerous and obvious and the guidelines which Kendall followed in his narrative poems are clearly similar to those laid down in Arnold's *Preface*. In the narratives Kendall moderates his tendency to a suffocating mass of descriptive flourishes. Description is tempered always by the narrative demands, yet it is effective and pleasing. His expression is kept reasonably, in Arnold's dictum, "in its right degree of prominence." It is because of this balance that Kendall's narrative poems (and especially "King Saul at Gilboa") stand up well to a close scrutiny of their structure and technique and as a result they leave the reader's poetical sense more highly gratified than do the lyrics.

V "The Voyage of Telegonus"

In "The Voyage of Telegonus"[26] Kendall moves from the Bible to the Homeric legends of Ulysses. Telegonus was the son of Ulysses and Circe, the sorceress of the island of Aeaea. When he reached manhood Telegonus went in search of his father but was shipwrecked on the coast of Ithaca, Ulysses' kingdom. There, to avoid starvation, he plundered and terrorized the inhabitants. When Ulysses and his son Telemachus (by Penelope) came to defend the property of their subjects against this unknown invader, Telegonus slew his father before he discovered his identity. Kendall's poem concludes with the funeral rites of Ulysses and the grief of his ill-fated son. The legend has Telegonus carry his father's body back to Aeaea, accompanied by Telemachus and Penelope. Telegonus married Penelope and they had a son Italus who gave his name to Italy.

This poem uncovers another link with Matthew Arnold, as A. D. Hope indicates in his discussion of Kendall in *Native Companions*. The slaying of an unknown son by his father was the theme of Arnold's great narrative poem, "Sohrab and Rustum," published in 1853. Such tragic tricks of fate had the same ready appeal to the sombre imagination of Kendall as they did to the elegiac fancy of Arnold. Kendall's poem was published first in the *Sydney Morning Herald*, June 11, 1866, with a long explanatory footnote from Lempriere's *Classical Dictionary* to help those colonial readers not well versed in the Classics.

The poem opens with a traditional declamation in carefully imitative Homeric tones. This initial set piece tells of the retribution that the gods exact from those who cross them. Telegonus, born "to be a scourge of Zeus," has his fate forecast in the opening lines:

> Ill fares it with the man whose lips are set
> To bitter themes and words that spite the gods:

> . . . his days shall know
> The plaintive front of Sorrow.

His journey to seek his father has been contrived by "black browed
Ares," the Greek god of the warlike spirit. Angered by Ulysses's victory on the plains of Troy, Ares, remembering an old prophecy "that
touched on Death and grief to Ithaca" and knowing too of the
legend of disaster ("sin beyond a name") that was attached to
Telegonus, planted in the young man's heart "longings for his
father's exiled face," longings that set him on his voyage to Ithaca.
Telegonus's shipwreck on the Ithacan coast is detailed in lines of
compact, descriptive power:

> . . . Sheer out
> The vessel drave; but three long moons the gale
> Moaned round; and swift strong streams of fire revealed
> The labouring rowers and the lightening surf,
> Pale watchers deafened of sonorous storm,
> And dripping decks and rents of ruined sails.
> Yea, when the hollow ocean-driven ship
> Wheeled sideways, like a chariot cloven through
> In hard hot battle, and the night came up
> Against strange headlands lying East and North,
> Behold a black wild wind with death to all
> Ran shoreward, charged with flame and thunder-smoke,
> Which blew the waters into wastes of white
> And broke the bark, as lightning breaks the pine.

Ares has his fellow god, Oceanus, rescue Telegonus from the
seething waters and he alone survives. For six days Telegonus is confined in a cave by the enormous seas but on the seventh morning,
drawn by the savoury aroma of cooking meats, he leaps out upon a
group of peasants preparing their morning food. The impact of this
dreadful apparition on the fear-struck rustics is admirably conveyed
by Kendall's lines. The action is controlled, and the effects obtained,
by a string of staccato phrases (one whole line is composed only of
monosyllables) which employ a succession of sibilants, interspersed
with the occasional plosive, to give the impression of speed, violent
movement and fear. The scene is completed with an analogy
between the fleeing peasants and far-blown Autumn leaves:

> At which the hunter, seized with sudden lust,
> Sprang up the crags, and, like a dream of Fear,

Leapt, shouting, at a huddled host of hinds
Amongst the fragments of their steaming food;
And, as the hoarse wood-wind in Autumn sweeps
To every zone the hissing latter leaves,
So, fleet Telegonus, by dint of spear
And strain of thunderous voice, did scatter these
East, South, and North.

Ithacan farmers carry the news of Telegonus's depredations to
Ulysses. Kendall moves crisply into the preparations the king makes
to meet the invader; the verse is full of action and movement. The
combat, when it comes, is monumentally brief, the dreadful result
achieved in only two blows, that of Ulysses evaded by Telegonus and
his own unerring, fatal reply:

The huge Ulysses, like a fire of fight,
Sprang sideways on the flying car, and drave
Full at the brass-clad warrior of the North
His massive spear; but fleet Telegonus
Stooped from the death, but heard the speedy lance
Sing like a thin wind through the steaming air,
Yet he, dismayed not by the dreadful foe —
Unknown to him — dealt out his strength, and aimed
A strenuous stroke at great Laertes' son,
Which missed the shield, but bit through flesh and bone,
And drank the blood, and dragged the soul from thence!

In Kendall's account of the grief of Telegonus when he discovers his
assailant's identity there is a pleasing restraint. Arnold's treatment of
the similar scene in "Sohrab and Rustum" has not satisfied
everyone. Although the reader is held entranced by Arnold's poetic
artistry the long, anguished exchanges between the dying Sohrab
and his horrified father tend to dissipate the emotional tension.
Kendall avoids this situation by viewing the tragedy through the
eyes of Ulysses's other son, Telemachus, the stoic, resigned witness
to the retribution of the gods upon ill-fated mortals. Superior as Arnold's poem undoubtedly is in imagery and language (there is no intention here to equate the two poems), there is little to choose
between either poet's peerless description of the moment of death.
Of Sohrab's death Arnold wrote:

. . . but the blood
Came welling from the open gash, and life

Flow'd with the stream; all down his cold white side
The crimson torrent ran, dim now and soil'd
Like the soil'd tissue of white violets
Left, freshly gather'd, on their native bank,
By children whom their nurses call with haste
Indoors from the sun's eye.

Kendall's analogy is equally striking:

. . . But lo, the life
Was like bright water spilt in sands of thirst,
A wasted splendour swiftly drawn away.

VI *"Ogyges"*

"Ogyges"[27] is less a narrative than a revelation of character and an analysis of attitudes to life and living. In Greek legend Ogyges was the king of Thebes in whose reign occurred the great flood that submerged Boeotia and part of Attica. Kendall attributes the flood to Zeus who plunged huge mountains into the sea causing the land to be engulfed by the resulting tidal wave:

When Zeus the Thunderer — broadly-blazing King —
Like some wild comet beautiful but fierce,
Leapt out of cloud and fire and smote the tops
Of black Ogygia with his red right hand,
At which great fragments tumbled to the Deeps —
The mighty fragments of a mountain-land —
And all the World became an awful Sea!

"Ogyges" was published in the *Colonial Monthly Magazine*, April, 1869, and included a few months later in the new volume. In a footnote to its first appearance Kendall admitted it to be "after the manner of Tennyson's *Tithonus* and Horne's *Orion*." "Ogyges" was not well received then or later. The link with Tennyson was deplored. "Ogyges," it was said, exposed Kendall's audacity for "daring to measure himself with some of the great masters of song"[28] and its graces were dismissed as nothing more than "plundered perfumes" from Tennyson. Most critics had already lost sight of Kendall's own admissions in the "Prefatory Sonnets." Sutherland included the poem among the "threadbare themes"[29] unsuitable for Australian poets. Most of this criticism was unproductive. Kendall was following standard poetic practice in using long-tried themes and a more penetrative analysis would have been to consider what his particular version had to offer. Modern critics have avoided the poem, possibly through disinterest, or perhaps deterred, as Reed suggests, by the profusion of classical references. But the essence of the poem can be easily separated from its classical origin. One can ignore the oddly named Theban king and recognise in the poem the archetypal figure of man, triumphing in spirit over the bondage of the body by old age. Around Ogyges is the stench of senility and decay. He is penned in a sea cave like some discarded old derelict, sunk in second childhood. "A hairless shadow in a lion's skin" he "mopes or mumbles, sleeps or shouts for glee / And shakes his sides — a cavern-hutted king!" From this torpor, however, he is always roused by the echoing horns of the nearby hunt. At such sounds his spirit breaks free from the lethargy of his aged body. Then he finds "a sudden stir, like life" about his feet and "tingling pulses" running through his frame. For Ogyges loved the hunt and its noises send his memory

> . . . wandering swiftly through the days
> When, like a springing cataract he leapt
> From crag to crag, the strongest in the chase
> To spear the lion, leopard, or the boar!

There is a fine image of old emotions stirred by the ever-exciting stimulation of wine upon his lips. The strength of the poem lies in these sharply etched pictures:

> The dear Demeter, splashed from heel to thigh
> With spinning vine-blood, often stoops to him
> To crush the grape against his wrinkled lips
> Which sets him dreaming of the thickening wolves
> In darkness, and the sound of moaning seas.

His evening reverie (filled with softer memories) is equally well-drawn:

> He sits as quiet as a thick-mossed rock,
> And dreameth in his cold old savage way
> Of gliding barges on the wine-dark waves,
> And glowing shapes, and sweeter things than sleep.

These twilight memories are of love and desire. The poem questions the value and worth of such transitory physical delights. In old age, when passion has been exhausted, is there anything worthwhile left?

The crux of Kendall's poem lies in the emergence of this central issue. The classical trappings fall away and the situation is revealed as one relevant to man in every age. The questions are asked of the old Theban King but the answers are universally applicable:

> Bethink you, doth the wan AEgyptian count
> This passion, wasting like an unfed flame,
> Of any worth now; seeing that his thighs
> Are shrunken to a span; and that the blood
> Which used to spin tumultuous down his sides
> Of life in leaping moments of desire,
> Is drying like a thin and sluggish stream
> In withered channels — think you, doth he pause
> For golden Thebe and her red young mouth?
> . . . .
> Ah, golden Thebe . . .
> If he could find a dream to comfort thee,
> He'd bring it . . .
> He'd count it sweetness past all sweets of love
> To die by thee — his life's end in thy sight.

Here is the affirmation of life. In spite of approaching death and the ageing body's inability to share any longer in the pleasures and fruits of life, there ought to be, in any man worthy of the name, a spiritual commitment to life, an affirming of its value, as it was in the past, lived in all its richness, and now, when all that is left of it is a thin "sluggish stream/In withered channels."

In Kendall's narratives, such as "Ogyges," there is an attractive quality of vigor and certainty that contrasts noticeably with the self-indulgent pathos of the lyrics. This quality — Kramer and Hope's "tense driving energy" — imparts an air of confident control which indicates both Kendall's relish for this type of verse and his remarkable, though seldom appreciated, talent for it.

VII *"Manasseh"*

In his final narrative, "Manasseh,"[30] published in the *Australian Journal* in Melbourne in 1870, Kendall returns to the Old Testament, the source of his King Saul narrative. Once established as King of Judah, Manasseh, who is believed to have ruled for fifty-five years, "let slip satanic passions" until the land "grew black/Beneath the shadow of despotic Sin." Kendall did not document Manasseh's apostasy in detail but the Old Testament tells that

He did what was evil in the sight of the Lord, according to the abominable
practices of the nations whom the Lord drove out before the people of Israel.
For he rebuilt the high places which Hezekiah his father had destroyed; and
he erected altars for Baal, and made an Asherah, as Ahab, King of Israel had
done, and worshipped all the host of heaven and served them . . . . And he
burnt his son as an offering, and practised soothsaying and augury, and dealt
with mediums and with wizards. He did much evil in the sight of the Lord
provoking him to anger.[31]

Kendall preferred to picture the desolation of Manasseh's rule:

> . . . the land that Moses strained
> On Nebo's topmost cone to see, grew black
> Beneath the shadow of despotic Sin
> That stalked on foot-ways dashed with human blood,
> And mocked high Heaven by audacious fires;
>
> . . . in the city of the wicked king
> A voice, like Abel's crying from the ground,
> Made sorrow of the broken evening winds,
> And darkness of the fair young morning lights,
> And silence in the homes of hunted men.

Retribution came with the attack by the Assyrian king, Esarhaddon.
Kendall follows the Chronicles, rather than 2 Kings, in having
Manasseh undergo a long imprisonment in Babylon, during which
he repents of his evil days, is rescued by divine intervention, restored
to his throne in Jerusalem, and spends his remaining years convert-
ing the people back to proper worship of the Lord. To this point the
poem is an effective narrative. Events are traced with economy and
precision and there are some attractive descriptive touches. But Kendall concludes, quite inexplicably, by reading a little homily to the
reader "whose sin/Lies heavy on his soul." He urges him to

> . . . find his way
> By paths of fire, as brave Manasseh did,
> Up to the white heights of a noble life.

Such sermonizing may have reflected Kendall's own guilty state of
mind at the time and may have been intended for self-flagellation. It
fits in too with the Victorian taste for pompous moralizing. But it
destroys altogether the value of the poem and Kendall's awareness of
this seems to be indicated by its absence from his second volume.

VIII   *Australian Narratives: "The Glen of Arrawatta"*

Kendall's two chief Australian narratives are "A Death in the Bush" and "The Glen of Arrawatta." "A Death in the Bush" was published first in 1860 as part of the fragmentary "The Australian Shepherd." It was then entitled "A Death Scene in the Bush." Discussion of it was given above in "The Australian Shepherd" section of *Poems and Songs*.

Like "A Death in the Bush," "The Glen of Arrawatta"[32] is a story from pioneering days. The tale of the lone settler murdered by the natives is commonplace in the frontier histories of developing countries but its horror never fades. Kendall's poem was first published in an eight-page booklet, together with a shorter poem, "Cui Bono?," by Hanson and Bennett, Sydney printers who were, after 1859, the publishers of the *Empire*. The booklet was undated and the poem was entitled "The Glen of The Whiteman's Grave." As the poem was not included in Kendall's first volume *Poems and Songs* it was probably written after that volume appeared in 1862. It was published in the second volume, *Leaves from Australian Forests*, with some minor changes in punctuation and wording and a new title, "The Glen of Arrawatta." By then Kendall had obviously become aware of one of Harpur's narrative poems of the same title which had appeared in the *Empire*, on March 17, 1857, and in a different, shorter form in the *Maitland Mercury* as far back as July 1, 1846. Both "Glen" poems give variations of the story of the white settler murdered by blacks. Harpur tells, in the first person, of coming across the lonely grave of a white man whose death he had heard of in bush conversations. He reconstructs the tragedy, expresses pity for the murdered man and sympathy for his grieving relatives. Kendall's is a more direct narration, in the third person, of the event itself, but, like Harpur's, concludes with sympathetic references to the bereaved relatives in England, whose remoteness from the tragedy is an admirable foil for the horrible actuality of the event itself. Kendall's poem also bears a marked similarity, in theme at least, to Harpur's well-known poem "The Creek of the Four Graves," which describes the murder of a group of settlers by aborigines. The latter poem appeared in 1853 in Harpur's book *The Bushrangers: A Play in Five Acts and Other Poems* but Kendall came to know of it only in 1862. "The Creek of the Four Graves" had a considerable influence on Kendall but neither his use of the same title as Harpur's "Glen" poem nor the murdered settler theme as in Harpur's "Creek" poem could be termed plagiarism. The choice of the same title (by no means an unusual one) seems to have been coincidence while the similarity in theme is not at all remarkable when one considers how common such incidents were in colonial life. In a letter to Harpur September 25, 1862, he stressed the response which "The Creek of the Four Graves" had aroused in him:

In the beginning of the present year . . . I secured a copy of the volume containing the "Bushrangers", and a noble poem headed "The Creek of the Four Graves." I *know* that a counterpart of Egremont [the survivor in the poem] has been with me in a grand evening Forest, where the fire looked "a wilder creature" than it would have seemed elsewhere, "because of the surrounding savageness"; and where we for a moment appeared to be part of a colossal picture, "hung in some vaster World." And I am *sure* we have watched the same solitary star which moved "so thoughtfully awake" over that vast Australian gloom. One of your old calumniators was frightened back to his native mind after hearing me read the "Creek of the Four Graves."

Kendall's problems with "The Glen of Arrawatta" followed him into later years. In 1879 the Art Union of Victoria chose it for a presentation volume. Kendall tried to dissuade them, probably a little embarrassed over the poem's origins and the apparent debt to Harpur, but they refused his alternative suggestions of "Wamberal" or "The Hut by the Black Swamp" (offered to them as "The Glen of Orimbah"). He added fifty-one lines to "The Glen of Arrawatta," made some minor alterations to the text, gave it yet another title, "Orara," and the Art Union published it in 1881.

This Australian narrative poem reinforces the impression gained from the biblical and classical poems that the narrative genre imposed a discipline on Kendall that the lyric could not. His task in the poem was to shape "a settler's story of the wild old times" and although the demands of the narrative did not preclude some descriptive flourishes they required that such description support and enhance the action. This conjunction of description and action occurs naturally and effectively, as these early lines indicate:

> For, in a far-off sultry Summer rimmed
> With thunder-cloud and red with forest-fires,
> All day, by ways uncouth and ledges rude,
> The wild men held upon a stranger's trail,

Which ran against the rivers and athwart
The gorges of the deep blue western hills.

And when a cloudy sunset, like the flame
In windy evenings on the Plains of Thirst
Beyond the dead banks of the far Barcoo,
Lay heavy down the topmost peaks, they came
With pent-in breath and stealthy steps, and crouched
Like snakes, amongst the grasses, till the Night
Had covered face from face and thrown the gloom
Of many shadows on the front of things.

There, in the shelter of a nameless glen
Fenced around by cedars and the tangled growths
Of blackwood stained with brown and shot with grey
The jaded white-man built his fire, and turned
His horse adrift amongst the water pools
That trickled underneath the yellow leaves
And made a pleasant murmur, like the brooks
Of England through the sweet autumnal noons.

The action itself proceeds with the measured deliberation of the inevitable. During the twilight the settler builds his shelter. As he toils
the blacks work closer and closer to the glen. Nature, chorus to the
tragedy, pours out insistent but unheeded warnings:

Then came the doleful owl; and evermore
The bleak morass gave out the bittern's call;
The plover's cry; and many a fitful wail
Of chilly omen, falling on the ear
Like those cold flaws of wind that come and go
An hour before the break of day.

A quiet interlude with strong ironic undercurrents follows. In the
growing darkness the settler smokes his evening pipe and revolves in
his mind "the primal questions of a squatter's life," problems of
pastures and water for his herds, the need to expand his run,
questions of profit and loss. Absorbed by the concerns of life he
makes plans which the next few hours are fated to bring to nothing.
In this interlude Kendall pictures the onward march of settlement
over the land, the squatter's herds now filling with "furious tumult"
the hills and valleys which before had known only "the marvellous
noise" of their own natural state. In the quiet of the peaceful

summer twilight the pensive squatter hears again this "marvellous noise," the voice of Nature, in much the same way as Wordsworth's "boy," mimicking the owls, caught its tones in the silences between the echoes of his calls

> Now, after Darkness, like a mighty spell
> Amongst the hills and dim dispeopled dells,
> Had brought a stillness to the soul of things,
> It came to pass that, from the secret depths
> Of dripping gorges, many a runnel-voice
> Came, mellowed with the silence, and remained
> About the caves, a sweet though alien sound:
> Now rising ever, like a fervent flute
> In moony evenings when the theme is love:
> Now falling, as ye hear the Sunday bells
> While hastening fieldward from the gleaming town.

The rising moon throws its light on a characteristic Australian scene — a forest carrying the scars of old bushfires:

> Black ghosts of trees, and sapless trunks that stood
> Harsh hollow channels of the fiery noise
> Which ran from bole to bole a year before.

To the colonial the bushfire was a constant source of wonder and amazement and writers vied with each other to picture its consuming fury for the enlightenment of readers back in England. Kendall's narrative is briefly sidetracked while he succumbs to the old lure of description for description's sake.

Finally the white man seeks his blanket. When he is asleep the savages strike. Of the settler's "hopeless struggles" Kendall wisely has little to say — he reserves the pathos for later scenes:

> So, after many moons, the searchers found
> The body mouldering in the mouldering dell
> . . . and buried it . . .
> There he lies and sleeps
> From year to year: in soft Australian nights.

The remainder of the poem takes up the traditional theme of friends and family at home in England watching for his return. It is an effective even if sterotyped finale. Kendall's English scenes, wrought from his imagination, are gracefully done. Changing seasons bring changing natural images, and the lines picture against these variations, the patient, unchanging vigil of the loved ones far away. In the end the years waste the watchers themselves as they wait for the one who sleeps in the Australian bush:

> But while the English Autumn filled her lap
> With faded gold, and while the reapers cooled
> Their flame-red faces in the clover grass,
> They looked for him at home; and when the frost
> Had made a silence in the morning lanes,
> And cooped the farmers by December fires,
> They looked for him at home: and through the days
> Which brought about the million-coloured Spring
> With moon-like splendours in the garden plots
> They looked for him at home: while Summer danced,
> A shining singer, through the tasselled corn,
> They looked for him at home. From sun to sun
> They waited. Season after season went,
> And Memory wept upon the lonely moors,
> And hope grew voiceless, and the watchers passed,
> Like shadows, one by one, away.

The changes made by Kendall for the Art Union of Victoria version of the poem were in two areas.[33] He added a dream for the sleeping white man, just before the attack: "A swift wild spirit from the sphere of Dreams/Slid down and took the weary wanderer's soul." In the dream his soul was carried over desolate oceans, past moaning bays "sad with the cry of shipwreck," past "bold New Zealand girt with lordly hills," to where it

> Beheld an English meadow starred with flowers
> And cool with deep green grasses where the kine
> Stand dreaming in a tender April sun.

The second addition gave a view of simultaneous events thousands of miles apart. From the grisly camp fire in the bush where the white man lay dying the scene was switched to the placid events of that same moment in his homeland. There, at supper (Kendall was poetically lax about variations from Greenwich Mean Time) the man's family talked

> With cheerful voices of the sturdy son
> Who left their thresholds seven years before

And crossed the seas, and under other skies
Found Fortune's fruit.

This insistence on giving Australian events an English affiliation is
typical of colonial attitudes and is surprisingly strong even in Kendall who had no personal ties with the old country. The Art Union
version was published less than twenty years before the end of the
nineteenth century, more than a hundred years after the First Settlement, a fact which indicates how long-preserved were those ties
between the colony and the parent country.

Kendall's Australian narratives have attracted over the years more
local interest and have generally been more popular than those
which he based on stories from the Bible and classical legend. This is
a natural and largely nonliterary reaction. Neither "A Death in the
Bush" nor "The Glen of Arrawatta" is ever likely to be considered an
Australian literary epic but they are worthwhile historically in that
they stand alongside "The Creek of the Four Graves," "The Sick
Stockrider," "The Man from Snowy River" and numerous other
narratives in the rich store of Australian pioneer legendry.

IX   *The Love Poems*

The broken love affair with Rose Bennett filled Kendall with a
bitter gloom that persisted for years. As a result the "Rose" poems
are infinitely sad, heavy with a hopeless sense of pain and loss. To
admit the deep significance of his love for Rose Bennett is not to dis-
parage his feelings for his wife. When he married Charlotte Rutter
the romance with Rose was in ruins and there is no doubt that Kendall loved his girl-bride and regarded his marriage vows as
sacrosanct. But with all this said, and as the love poems so ex-
pressively tell, Rose Bennett held a place in his heart that was hers
alone.

Most of the poems concerned with Rose appeared in 1869,
although they could have been written a year or so earlier. The best
known of the group is "Rose Lorraine," which Kendall included in
his second volume *Leaves From Australian Forests;* however, the
climactic poem of the series is "At Nightfall," which did not appear
in that book, being published separately in April, 1870. "At Nightfall"[34] contains Melbourne references. These could indicate that it
was written too late for inclusion in *Leaves,* although its absence is
probably attributable to its deeply personal and private nature. After
it abandons its conventional setting of the gloomy twilight and the

sombre lover's self-pitying glances towards his thin greying hair, his "mournful sense" of "growing old before his time," the poem becomes a simple, moving picture of a life made desolate by the loss of love. It recalls the bittersweet memories of days filled with "strength and love and joy and hope":

> The soft dead days before him, one by one,
> Float, dim as Banquo's issue in the play;
> And these with thin sad voices seem to say —
> We *too* were part of thee; we *each* are waifs —
> Pale perished waifs of thee, and Love and Youth!

Overcome with the pain of such memories the poet "makes a darkness with his hollowed hands/About his faded face" and begs for oblivion:

> He fain would find some Lethe which would bring
> That state of rest and great forgetfulness
> In which the Past with all its lights and shade
> Is wholly drowned and nothing comes to vex
> The soul with hints of sorrow born of death,
> Or broken hopes, or disappointed loves.

Kendall found, for a time, his own kind of oblivion in alcohol. There has never been any attempt to link his drinking with his lost love of "Rose Lorraine," but these lines may possess some biographical significance. It was certainly not until after his parting from her in 1867 that he became an alcoholic and Kendall would not have been the first forlorn lover to try to cure a broken heart by drowning his sorrows.

Kendall has never written more feelingly than in the poem's final lines which tell of his utterly hopeless, heartbroken misery:

> Ah, Love! there is no passion like the first:
> I feel it when I breathe your slow sweet name,
> I know it when I hear the songs you loved,
> It burns me when I pass you in the street;
> In all my dreams your shadow floats about,
> In all my walks your presence fills the time,
> In all my verse there is a trace of you;
> And since our alienation I have felt
> That sense of loss which never leaves a man,
> But kills his pleasure in the glad green earth,

And spills his love for God's most perfect days,
And makes him tired and sick of all that is.

By comparison with "At Nightfall" the better-known "Rose
Lorraine"[35] is almost a trifle, born of sentiment rather than passion.
"At Nightfall" came six months after "Rose Lorraine," six months of
mental and physical disintegration in Melbourne. By that time Kendall's defences were completely down, his morale at rock bottom, his
sense of loss absolute. By then, as "At Nightfall" reveals, there was
no point in dalliance, nothing to be gained by disguising the pain.
Only occasionally in "Rose Lorraine" is the pain of "At Nightfall"
present, and then it is met and countered by the simple device of
self-discipline. When the sense of loss overwhelms him, in the
"stormy nights" and "times of rain", he turns "towards the wall" to
luxuriate momentarily in grief and tears, but for the most part he can
present a brave front to the world. There is no relief in "At Nightfall" — he is beyond self-discipline, consumed with heartache that
" . . . makes him tired and sick of all that is." In "Rose Lorraine"
there is distress but no agony. As often as the poet hovers on the
brink of despair because of his lost love there comes a succession of
querulous complaints and accusations — 'he suffered much," "his
fate was worst," "the wilful face that hurt me so" — that reduce it
almost to a stereotyped lover's lament. The last verse, with its sentimental treasuring of a "keepsake," gives the poem a romantic aura
that readers have found, predictably enough, pleasantly attractive.

> I keep a faded ribbon string
> You used to wear about your throat;
> And of this pale, this perished thing
> I think I know the threads by rote.
> God help such love! To touch your hand,
> To loiter where your feet might fall,
> You marvellous girl, my soul would stand
> The worst of hell — its fires and all.

The first three sonnets of the "Twelve Sonnets" in *Leaves from
Australian Forests* belong to the "Rose" love poems. Two of them,
"A Mountain Spring" and "By A River," were published in the
Australasian on June 12, 1869; the third, "Laura," in the same
newspaper four days later.

"A Mountain Spring"[36] describes a favorite Kendall haunt, "a still
bright pool" nestling in a secluded mountain dell, untouched by the

violence of lashing storms that beat against the "fire-rifted summits." "Peace," he says "hath an altar there." So, it seems, has love. By the edge of the limpid waters he revolves memories of "gracious nights whose lips with flowers are sweet," nights of "loved and lost repose." The crystal depths give him back the face that is always in his thoughts, "that faithless face of Rose."

"By A River"[37] admits that the vision of Rose, with her "red ripe mouth and brown luxurious eyes," gives his soul no peace. Even the "green and golden-hearted beauty" of Nature that graces the river banks gains added loveliness and brings added grief by reflecting back to him "her marvellous face." It is a simple, lovely sonnet, revealing just how deft and graceful is Kendall's touch when he follows the Muse's ageless advice to "look in thy heart and write":

> But red ripe mouth and brown luxurious eyes
> Of her I love, by all your sweetness shed
> In far fair days, on one whose memory flies
> To faithless lights and gracious speech gainsaid,
> I pray you, when yon river-path I tread,
> Make with the woodlands some soft compromise
> Lest they should vex me into fruitless sighs
> With visions of a woman's gleaming head!
> For every green and golden-hearted thing
> That gathers beauty in that shining place
> Beloved of beams and wooed by wind and wing
> Is rife with glimpses of her marvellous face;
> And in the whispers of the lips of Spring
> The music of her lutelike voice I trace.

"Laura"[38] was entitled "Rose" in the autograph manuscript, now held by Archibishop Reed, and when published first in the *Australasian*. Deference for his wife's feelings probably led Kendall to change the title in the *Leaves* volume. Where "By A River" is natural and spontaneous, "Laura" is contrived and artificial, as poor a poem as Kendall wrote. "Lady of the flower-soft face" is a pale substitute for the strong physical impact of "red ripe mouth and brown luxurious eyes." The trite image of the bereft poet as "a thin pale Figure" awakens none of the compassion felt for the previous sonnet's picture of a man so desperately hurt that he averts his eyes from natural beauty lest he see mirrored there the face of his lost love. The line, "She left me, fleeting like a fluttered dove" is further evidence of Kendall's hopeless infatuation in the lyric form for the

96   HENRY KENDALL

empty alliterative phrase. This infatuation reaches the peak of abandonment in the overwrought images of the final lines:

> But I would have a moment of her breath,
> So I might taste the sweetest sense thereof,
> And catch from blossoming, honeyed lips of love,
> Some faint, some fair, some dim delicious death.

"Laura" contains many of the characteristics — and all of the faults — of the Courtly Love sonnets of a long past age.

"After Parting"[39] is one of the "Twelve Sonnets" in the *Leaves* volume but it can have no reference to Rose Bennett. It was published as early as 1863. A reader unaware of that date would imagine it to be one of the group of sonnets just discussed, or at least to have had its origin in a broken love affair. Such was not the case. Kendall was involved at the time in a mild, desultory flirtation with Anne Hopkins. In a letter to him she sought factual details of the poem but Kendall was able to reply (July 10, 1863) that the lady of "After Parting" was only a poetical creation, and the "passion" which the poem describes had not yet been experienced. Kendall's inclination for anticipating the sadness of a lost and broken love, rather than the joy and fulfilment of a happy love, is indicative, as were the early *Poems and Songs*, of the melancholy bent of his nature. The opening lines of "After Parting," which are similar in tone to "By A River," are splendidly forlorn:

> I cannot tell what change hath come to you
> To vex your splendid hair. I only know
> One grief: the passion left betwixt us two,
> Like some forsaken watchfire, burneth low.
> 'Tis sad to turn and find it dying so
> Without a hope of resurrection!

In contrast to the "Rose" poems there is only one love poem to Kendall's wife, Charlotte. This is the brief, "For My Darling Lottie"[40] which was not published until 1898. It was a poem sent by Kendall to Charlotte Rutter in January, 1868, not long before she became his wife. The lines were accompanied by the following note: "For my darling Lottie to whom a passionate love and its ceaseless longings are given. My bright pet cannot question the power of that affection. Let it be her cloak to shelter her for ever and ever."

The different intensity of his feelings can be gauged by the phrase "bright pet" and the gentle tone he adopts. The poem is a tender, loving address, but it lacks the emotional tension of the verses to Rose Bennett. Several other poems contain tributes to his wife but they are not love poems. The "Dedication" at the beginning of *Leaves from Australian Forests* tells of his gratitude to her in the difficult Melbourne days and calls her "my bright best friend." In "Araluen,"[41] a poem mourning the death of their first child, there is a stronger note of personal affection:

> Girl, whose hand at God's high altar in the dear dead year I pressed,
> Lean your stricken head upon me: this is still your lover's breast!

In "On A Street,"[42] there is grief for the distress he brought her, the "patient, pure young wife," but none of the intense man-woman relationship which characterizes the "Rose" poems.

X *"In Memoriam"*

The practice of favoring deceased public figures, or relatives, or friends, with memorial eulogies in verse, although routine in colonial literature, has not survived into modern times. There are many such poems among Kendall's collected verse. Several of them are of some historical interest, adding as they do to our meager knowledge of the people involved — people such as Charles Harpur, Daniel Deniehy and J. L. Michael. In the best of Kendall's "In Memoriam" verses there is, too, some sincerely expressed and technically accomplished poetry. Mostly, however, they are unimpressive poems, written almost as set pieces to an established formula. Poetry written to prescription is unlikely to possess much merit and Kendall's is no exception. The memorial verses to L. H. Lavenu, W. Vincent Wallace, W. V. Wild, Edward Butler, N. D. Stenhouse, and to a lesser extent Robert Parkes, the son of Sir Henry Parkes, are of little worth. Those in memory of Harpur, Deniehy and Michael are interesting because of their subjects while those to Archdeacon McEncroe and Adam Lindsay Gordon are the best of this rather artificial and depressing poetic genre.

The Harpur poem[43] is disappointing. One looks for well-founded critical insight and deep personal familiarity when Kendall writes of his dead brother poet, for he was one of the few people who should have known Harpur well. But the Harpur who emerges from the

memorial verses is not the Harpur that exists in either the few letters
that he wrote in response to Kendall's many, or in the poems that his
reputation is built on. Kendall has allowed his imagination, as so
often happens in eulogy, to construct its own idealized image. The
poem begins with a sweeping assessment of the influence of the
natural environment on Harpur's poetry:

> Where Harpur lies, the rainy streams,
> And wet hill-heads, and hollows weeping,
> Are swift with wind, and white with gleams,
> And hoarse with sounds of storms unsleeping.
>
> Fit grave it is for one whose song
> Was tuned by tones he caught from torrents,
> And filled with mountain-breaths, and strong
> Wild notes of falling forest-currents.

Harpur did have a strong attachment to the Australian landscape, especially for the kind of country the poem describes, the Hawkesbury
river country where he grew up. It provided him with some of his
prime poetic impulses, for example, "A Storm in the Mountains"
and "A Midsummer Noon in the Australian Forest"; but Harpur's
"song" was tuned by numerous other, and more important, influences, influences which sprang from his character and
background and the social and political situations of the day. In
stressing Harpur's "fellowship with gorge and glen" Kendall is in-
vesting him with attitudes more characteristically Kendall's own.
There are other glib, and faulty, observations. Harpur's "speech of
sweetness" is inaccurate, for he was no natural lyrist; he would have
scorned to have been thought "serene as light"; and "delights of
Men were his delights" is hard to justify. Harpur shared few, if any,
delights with others and he strongly deplored the *common* delight of
the day — materialism — detesting his fellows who always sought
"money's worth" or believed that "earthly gain alone is fair." The
poem does however acknowledge Harpur's importance to Australian
poetry and this was one of the rare occasions when recognition was
given to him. Kendall saw Harpur as the first poet, "whose hands at-
tuned the Harp Australian," a judgment which was not taken up by
other critics for several generations but which, in modern times has
continued to gain more and more approval.

Daniel Deniehy, a man of infinite promise, noted in his lifetime as
a writer, orator and public figure, died at the age of thirty-seven with

his great talent squandered through alcoholism. Kendall wrote of him in an article, "About Some Men of Letters in Australia" in the *Australian Journal*, October, 1869:

I fell in with him about a year or so before his death, at a stage when his physical and mental powers were all but gone. Nevertheless there were some flashes of the old light in him even then. When the spirit came upon him, as it did on rare and fortunate occasions, his wasted face was wont to become like the face of one glorified. I have been in his society in moments when his countenance, plain in repose, has caught a fire and beauty that looked like phases of actual transfiguration.[44]

In memory of Deniehy Kendall wrote two poems — "Deniehy's Dream" in 1866 (unpublished until 1920) and "In Memoriam — Daniel Henry Deniehy," published in the *Australasian*, March 23, 1867 about eighteen months after Deniehy's death. "Deniehy's Dream"[45] is a lame, halting set of verses, giving only the barest glimpse of what that dream might be. Kendall probably put it by as unfit for publication. "In Memoriam — Daniel Henry Deniehy"[46] is little better. It rebukes those (Kendall among them) who failed to help Deniehy when he most needed it:

Take the harp, but very softly, for the friend who grew so old
Through the hours we would not hear of — nights we would not fain behold!

The poem is overlaid with continual personification and extended landscape imagery; there are few references to Deniehy himself. After the lines quoted above there is no further comment on Deniehy and his travail until the end of the poem where he is described as "one who, failing, suffered all the poet's pain."

The poem "James Lionel Michael"[47] was published in Sheridan Moore's *Life and Genius of James Lionel Michael* in 1868. There had been a time when Kendall had needed Michael. In 1863 he had written "Lines to J. L. Michael"[48]:

Go on, I shall follow,
'Tis well you should lead;
For teacher, without you,
I shake like a reed.

. . . .
At your feet will I listen
To all you can say;

> For my thoughts, this morning,
> Were yours yesterday.

By 1865 he had outgrown that need. He wrote: "The more I know of
men and books the less faith I have in Mr. Michael's abilities. He
appears to me to be a smart chatterbox who has a happy knack of
persuading everybody that he knows everything. He is undoubtedly
clever but not original in the least particular. I have never heard him
say a beautiful thing yet that was his own."[49] After Michael's death
his attitude was kinder. He made allowances for human frailty, of
which Michael had his share, and was sympathetic toward the
hapless friend who had often brought misfortune upon his own head.
Michael was one "who knew the friendless face/Sorrows show," one
"too apt to faint and fail," one whom care bound "with an iron
band." His death had clearly healed the rift between them:

> Be his rest the rest he sought
> Calm and deep
> Let no wayward word or thought
> Vex his sleep.

    John McEncroe was the Dean of the Roman Catholic Cathedral of
Sydney. His death in 1868, together with Harpur's and Michael's,
made that year an especially gloomy one for Kendall. "In
Memoriam Archdeacon McEncroe"[50] is a beautiful eulogy. It is not a
poem of grief, the lines glowing with quiet confidence that the dead
priest enjoys the "sweet repose" that lies "upon the just." Death,
which so often in Kendall is linked with the bitterness and struggle
associated with life, is for this saintly man an experience of serenity
and fulfillment. The moment holds no pain, no grief, no fear. The
quiet, graceful cadences of the opening lines fall upon the ear as
gently as the words of a prayer:

> A Father gone! In quiet skies
> The final ray died sweet and fair
> Which closed his consecrated eyes
> As with a prayer.
>
> Life left him like a faultless psalm
> That mounts and mingles with the stars;
> And one more soul has reached the calm
> Past woes and wars.

This poem's superiority over Kendall's other memorial verses is due to his awareness of the beauty of the character of the man he mourns. McEncroe's character *is* the poem; his gentleness toward "his suffering peers" of all religious creeds, his own peerless faith that sustained him when those about him wavered "like seaside reeds," his patient endurance of his own "tests of suffering," and the instinctive humanity that lay at the root of his saintliness.

A week after Adam Lindsay Gordon's suicide Kendall's poem, "The Late Mr. A. L. Gordon: In Memoriam"[51] was published in the *Australasian*, July 2, 1870. The two poets were not close friends. They had met occasionally at the Yorick gatherings and there is the traditional story of their having spent most of Gordon's last afternoon drinking together. There is not much evidence that they knew or respected each other's work, although Gordon did praise Kendall's "The Hut by the Black Swamp" in one of the few letters known to pass between them.[52] Kendall's own position in 1870 was probably as desperate as Gordon's — his efforts to make a living for his family by his pen had failed: he blamed himself for the death of his daughter, Araluen; his energy and drive were sapped by alcoholism. Something of the shadow that lay across his own life finds expression in his memorial to Gordon. There is almost a trace of envy for the dead man — he is "at rest," with the struggle over, basking, as it were, in the admiration and respect of his fellows, tendered too late but welcome nevertheless.

The first half of the poem is the best of Kendall's memorial verses. The blank verse, straightforward, simple and spendidly eloquent, imparts the solemnity and strength necessary for elegiac poetry. This is especially true of the well-known opening stanza:

> At rest! Hard by the margin of that sea
> Whose sounds are mingled with his noble verse,
> Now lies the shell that never more will house
> The fine, strong spirit of my gifted friend.
> Yea, he who flashed upon us suddenly
> A shining soul with syllables of fire
> Who sang the first great songs these lands can claim
> To be their own; the one who did not seem
> To know what royal place awaited him
> Within the Temple of the Beautiful,
> He passed away; and we who knew him, sit
> Aghast in darkness, dumb with that great grief,
> Whose stature yet we cannot comprehend;

> While over yonder churchyard, hearsed with pines,
> The nightwind sings its immemorial hymn,
> And sobs above a newly-covered grave.

The second stanza cites Gordon as the perfect example of English chivalry and in true eulogistic fashion declares him the paragon of virtue — a judgment that not all who knew Gordon would share. In the final stanzas the strong tone breaks, bathos and sentimentality creep in, and insipid "poetic" phrases replace the terse simplicity of the opening lines. Kendall casts himself in the role of a literary Sir Bedivere, left to lament the passing not only of Gordon but of J. L. Michael and Charles Harpur, the other leading graces of the colonial literary scene. This results in the final emphasis of the poem being laid on Kendall himself rather than the tragic waste of Gordon's death:

> To Adam Lindsay Gordon, I who laid
> Two years ago on Lionel Michael's grave
> A tender leaf of my regard: yea I
> Who culled a garland from the flowers of song
> To place where Harpur sleeps; I, left alone,
> The sad disciple of a shining band
> Now gone! to Adam Lindsay Gordon's name
> I dedicate these lines . . .
> And having wove and proffered this poor wreath,
> I stand to-day as lone as he who saw
> At nightfall through the glimmering moony mists,
> The last of Arthur on the wailing mere,
> And strained in vain to hear the going voice.

CHAPTER 4

Kendall's Poetry:
The Final Period

I Songs from the Mountains

A count of Kendall's published poems in the years immediately following the publication of *Leaves from Australian
Forests* in 1869, shows the impact of alcoholism and its attendant
personal problems upon his literary achievements. Only nine poems
can be traced to 1870, his final year in Melbourne. These included
the bitter love poem, "At Nightfall," the memorial verses to Adam
Lindsay Gordon, and "Euterpe — An Ode to Music," the poem
commissioned for the opening of the Melbourne Town Hall on
August 9, 1870. A mere five poems are attributed (none with any certainty) to the following year, 1871, when, back in Sydney, he un-
derwent his first treatment in the Gladesville Asylum. In 1872 and
1873 there was no poetry. Several later poems were sub-titled
"Written in the shadow of 1872," but they were composed some
time after the events of that year. Toward the end of 1873 his
restoration under the care of the Fagan family at Brisbane Water
began, but he shunned any kind of literary activity. From Gosford,
November 19, 1874, when his recovery was almost complete, he
tried to justify his attitude to J. Sheridan Moore:

The fact is I hate the sight of a pen. I may from time to time scribble off a
squib or a prose trifle but as to more serious work — bah! I had quite enough
of it during the weary years between 1869 and 1874 .... Why should I
bother and work out my brains for a shadow? Did Harpur acquire a reputation by his writings? Did Michael and Gordon with all their belief in
themselves? If they failed what right have I to expect success? And what,
after all, is success of the kind worth? Nothing. Give me the boring life and
let the Gods go hang!

Later at Camden Haven, May 17, 1876, he declared: "I rarely ever
write now .... My promise has been kept. I have left the fields of
literature for ever."

Kendall, was, as usual, dramatizing a little. He had begun writing poetry again in 1874, his letters to P. J. Holdsworth showing that "The Voice in the Wild Oak" was composed in June and "Narrara Creek" in September of that year.[1] In December, 1875, he sent a further three poems to Holdsworth, one of which was "Mooni." Except for "Galatea" all the poems included in his final volume, *Songs from the Mountains*, were written from 1874 onwards, with the bulk of them coming after his reunion with his family in 1876. His success in the *Sydney Morning Herald's* poetry competition associated with the International Exhibition of 1879 revitalized his literary ambitions and led him to think of a third volume of poems. The financial failures of his previous two books had made him wary of the expense involved so he sought expert opinion of his prospects. F. W. Ward, then editor of the *Sydney Mail*, suggested a subscription volume based on four hundred subscribers. Kendall began negotiations for the new book in July, 1880, with publisher William Maddock of Sydney. The letters to Maddock reveal a new, mercenary strain in Kendall; he kept all the business arrangements under his own control, watching hawklike over the subscription money as it came through. His instructions to Maddock were unsentimental and hardheaded: "There are some relatives of mine that you may have heard of. Do not entertain applications not endorsed by me," *and* "I do not care to give 'tick' to Government clerks — so make these fellows pay. Some of them are good marks — but treat all alike."[2] *Songs from the Mountains* came from the printer on December 16, 1880, and was almost immediately withdrawn. W. B. Dalley, receiving an early copy for review, warned Maddock that one satirical skit, "The Song of Ninian Melville," could be the subject of a libel action. Maddock scoured Sydney in a frantic effort to recall all copies, excised the offending poem and pasted in a new one, "Christmas Creek"; he then reissued the book in January, 1881. Because of these curious happenings *Songs from the Mountains* is a collector's item. It exists in three different forms — the original issue, containing "The Song of Ninian Melville," published in December, 1880; the original issue with the pages 145 - 152 excised, "Christmas Creek" pasted in and a new table of contents; and the new issue with no indication of any alterations, appearing in January, 1881. Aided by some publicity from these events the book sold rapidly. After three months one thousand copies had been sold and Kendall, in spite of the additional costs involved in the "Ninian Melville" mix-up, made a profit of more than eighty pounds.

Songs from the Mountains was well received. Sutherland wrote, in October, 1882:

Between this new book and the former there is a wide gulf fixed. It is possible to recognise the old Kendall in it, but only barely possible. The sentimental doggerel of the "Euroclydon" class is altogether absent, and there is an infusion of vigor that gives a new ring to the verse. "Mary Rivers," "Hy-Brazil," "Mooni," "Narrara Creek," "Araluen," "Names Upon a Stone," and "After Many Years," are in most respects superior to anything in the "Leaves from an Australian Forest" [*sic*].[3]

Sutherland's judgments are difficult to accept. Earlier in the same article he had highly praised *Leaves from Australian Forests*, assessing some of the *Leaves* poems as the equal of Wordsworth and Milton. Yet the new poems he considered "superior to anything" in *Leaves*. Logically then the poems of the final volume are much superior to Wordsworth and Milton. Judgments such as these have done much to discredit colonial critical values. W. B. Dalley in his review of *Songs from the Mountains* in the *Sydney Morning Herald*, January 12, 1881, praised the book for its "power and beauty . . . imaginative tenderness, emotional fervour and . . . easy command of rich and forcible English." This early critical approval, and perhaps the fact that it was his final volume, have led to the widely held assumption that *Songs from the Mountains* contains Kendall's best poetry. A close examination of the poems does not support that assumption. There is some improvement in the lyrics, most of which are still strongly biographical, but there is a lack of substance in many of the other poems. The intellectual tone of the book is pitched at a lower level than either of the previous volumes — deliberately so, according to Kendall's comments to G. G. McCrae: "The book will disappoint you but the verses, that eclectics like you will sneer at, are the ones that Tom, Jack and Harry admire. I want to make friends of these gentlemen with a view to the recovery of my outlay."[4] This attempt to win popularity with the general reader by the flippant, derogatory, aboriginal verses, by the trivial pieces such as "Rover" and "Bob," by the character sketches "Jim the Splitter," "Bill the Bullock Driver," "Billy Vicars" and by "Kingsborough," a poor attempt at a racing ballad, shows a new side of Kendall. His earlier books had been entirely devoted to the earnest expression of his poetic art. With an eye now on the prospects of financial reward he abandons the role of serious poet and adopts the pose of sardonic observer of the whole colonial scene. His jibes at the blacks and the

loudmouthed, ignorant type of Australian are not poetry at all. They are satirical skits, crudely witty, bitingly sarcastic and slangily colloquial, a combination much to the taste of the general reading public of the day.

Songs from the Mountains is also the thinnest of Kendall's three books, containing only thirty-five poems. Since his previous volume, eleven years before, he had accumalated no more than seventy poems from which to select for the new book. Except for "At Nightfall" and "The Song of Ninian Melville," which were omitted for reasons already mentioned, and the memorial verses to Gordon which had received wide coverage a decade earlier, the rejected poems were of poor quality. The final volume is the most individualistic of the three, many of the poems being fugitive pieces that form no overall pattern of theme or thought. The most important group, lyrics such as "Mooni" and "Narrara Creek," is autobiographical, commencing with Kendall's regretful meditations about events leading up to the "Shadow of 1872" and climaxing in "To a Mountain" where at last a new, strong note of hope emerges. Another definite group is the collection of satirical verses about the aboriginals and bush characters. Kendall's best satire, "The Gagging Bill," was unfortunately, but predictably, excluded from the volume, together with several minor poems in the same vein, for example, "A Psalm for the Conventicle" and "Things I don't like to see."[5] The final volume also included his two competition pieces, the prize winning Sydney International Exhibition poem and the unsuccessful Melbourne International Exhibition attempt. Perhaps the most interesting individual poem is "Beyond Kerguelen,"[6] the bleak south seascape that had remained in his memory from his days at sea as a cabin boy. It is an intriguing and rather irritating poem. Some of Kendall's best imagery is displayed in it and it gives the impression that he is about to break through into successful, descriptive lyricism. But it is spoiled by the repetitiveness of its theme — the barren desolation of the south lands — which Kendall tries to overcome by simply inventing new ways of describing the same scene in verse after verse. The device of ending alternate lines with the same phrase is an interesting experiment, but the poem is too long to carry this without losing effect.

II   *"The Shadow of 1872"*

Before Kendall could achieve the spiritual peace evident in the dedicatory poem "To a Mountain" he had first to admit and exorcise

the guilt of the past. He did this in three poems that he subtitled "Written in the shadow of 1872," namely, "The Voice in the Wild Oak," "Narrara Creek," and "Mooni," and in two others of this final period, "Araluen" and "On a Street." Guilt, however, is not the sole emotion of these poems. Through them runs a strong strain of self-pity. They veer constantly from chagrin and remorse about his own behavior to complaints of victimization and lack of understanding. The first of the poems, "The Voice in the Wild Oak,"[7] written in June, 1874, before "Narrara Creek" and "Mooni," traces back to a much earlier poem "The Wail in the Native Oak,"[8] November, 1861, which in turn was inspired by Harpur's appealing lyric "The Voice of the Swamp Oak." In *The Poetical Works of Henry Kendall* Archbishop Reed gives an account of the origin of the 1874 poem written at Brisbane Water: "In 1938 C. H. Bertie informed me that George Fagan told him that he and Kendall were lying one day on the ground propped up against the tree. At that time there were many oaks growing along the banks of the river. While they lay there Kendall suddenly exclaimed, 'George, I've been listening to the voices of the oaks; they are just like human voices.' Next day he wrote the poem."[9] In the opening verse Kendall recalls the 1861 poem, contrasting those days, "full flowered with hours of grace," with the present which is "sad with sighs." He attributes the failure of the first poem to capture and interpret the voice of the oak to his poetic inexperience:

> I wrote a song in which I strove
> To shadow forth thy strain of woe,
> Dark widowed sister of the grove —
> Twelve wasted years ago.

> But youth was then too young to find
> Those high authentic syllables
> Whose voice is like the wintering wind
> By sunless mountain fells.

This new attempt he believes is also certain to fail. The griefs of the past few years (admittedly self-inflicted) have dulled his "fine first sense/of Beauty" and so diminished his rapport with nature that he feels incapable of success.

> But I who am that perished soul
> Have wasted so these powers of mine,

That I can never write that whole
Pure, perfect speech of thine,
Some lord of words august, supreme,
The grave, grand melody demands:
The dark translation of thy theme
I leave to other hands.

There is much self-commiseration. He describes himself as ". . . one whose hair was shot with gray/By Grief instead of Time." He claims not to have to play the traditional poetic role of singing "imaginary pain" — his is the real, and intolerable, "punishment of Cain." P. J. Holdsworth, to whom Kendall had sent the poem from Gosford, was convinced of the therapeutic value of poetry for him at that critical stage, and obviously remonstrated with him over the grief and guilt of the poem. Kendall replied: "As regards the tone of the *Native Oak*, I cannot help it. You know something of my personal history; and you will hardly say that it has been a very happy one. To the end of the chapter, my expression will take colour from the great grief which is making an old man of me. As to my complaints about the wane of power, I have good reason to make them. The old Passion is past kindling now."[10] Having asserted his incapacity to interpret the oak's "grand old theme" he goes on to attempt exactly that. The voice of the oak is given embodiment in several gloomy but apt images. It is the voice of a "Dream - haunted spirit, doomed to be/Imprisoned, crampt in bands of bark,/For all eternity," or it belongs to "Some wan Tithonus of the wood/White with immeasurable years." Or it may be the voice of the oak's soul, which, stirred by the memory of some dreadful past deed, sends its cries "like maledictions, shrill" curdling along the glen. In less disturbed times, as in the amiable springtime, the oak's voice is tranquil, calm with the peace that comes with the resigned and dignified acceptance of sorrows. These lines, which carry an implicit analogy between Kendall and the oak, reflect Kendall's theatrical view of himself as the aggrieved and noble sufferer, bearing stoically his burden of grief.

All three "Shadow of 1872" poems are set against the background of the Brisbane Water country. The strange, almost grim, beauty of this area and its fascination for him, is captured in the rich but cramped prose of his articles in *Town and Country Journal*, entitled "Arcadia in our midst," February 23 and March 6, 1875. "Narrara Creek"[11] tells of this precipitous, picturesque landscape where the creek, at first a bright, newborn thing, cascades over waterfalls and hurtles through steep gorges and gloomy valleys out onto the broad flat plain. There, its youthful frolic over, it settles into the sedate maturity of a stately stream. The leaping rhythms of the first verse reflect the hectic movement of turbulent mountain water:

> From the rainy hill-heads where, in starts and in spasms,
> Leaps wild the white torrent from chasms to chasms —
> From the home of bold echoes whose voices of wonder
> Fly out of blind caverns struck black by high thunder —
> Through gorges august in whose nether recesses
> Is heard the far psalm of unseen wildernesses —
> Like a dominant spirit, a strong-handed sharer
> Of spoil with the tempest, comes down the Narrara.

A more measured, deliberate movement is achieved by lengthened vowel and consonant sounds to picture the leisurely movement of the river of the plains:

> It broadens, and brightens, and thereupon marches
> Above the stream-sapphires and under green arches
> With the rhythm of majesty — careless of cumber —
> Its might in repose and its fierceness in slumber —
> Till it beams on the plains where the wind is a bearer,
> Of words from the sea to the stately Narrara!

Against the background of the attractive stream and magnificent scenery Kendall makes a further appraisal of his life. His tone is rueful — he has spoiled his golden chances. The refrain "too late" sums up his depressed state of mind. In the published version of the poem he blames himself:

> What life the gods gave me — what largess I tasted —
> The youth thrown away and the faculties wasted!
> I might, as thou seest, have stood in high places
> Instead of in pits where the brand of disgrace is.

In another version of the poem, the Mitchell Library manuscript, he criticises his wife: "I might have been different — happy and human,/Had the woman I loved been more like a woman." "Narrara Creek," although written in 1874, was not published until May 18, 1878, in *Sydney Once a Week*. By then Kendall had lost the bitter sense of betrayal that he had felt after his wife had left him and could see his own fault more clearly. Hence the variation in the verses. The poem is not without traces of self-pity, occasional querulous tilts at the world at large and womankind in particular. There is no sign of the serenity that was to come in 1880 with "To a Mountain" for Kendall, in 1874, believed his life to be still an unhappy mess. "Narrara Creek" does show, however, that he was coming to terms with his own guilt and that the healing process had begun.

Technically, the poem is not greatly superior to the landscape lyrics of *Leaves from Australian Forests*. In the early portion, where Kendall strives for descriptive impact, there is still the tendency to overembellish, to crowd the lines with dramatic phrases, and to revive the old flow of mesmerising alliteration. In the second half, personal reminiscence reduces this striving for picturesque effects and the verse flows more fluently and easily. In the final lines the Kendall "bell-birds" syndrome reappears and the pretentious, sentimental, singsong catchiness that Kendall mistook for lyricism takes over:

> But the face of thy river — the torrented power
> That smites at the rock while it fosters the flower —
> Shall gleam in my dreams with the summer-look splendid,
> And the beauty of woodlands and waterfalls blended;
> And often I'll think of far forested noises,
> And the emphasis deep of grand sea-going voices;
> And turn to Narrara the eyes of a lover
> When the sorrowful days of my singing are over.

"Mooni,"[12] written in 1875, a year after Kendall had left Brisbane Water for Camden Haven, recalls the time of happiness before "sin and shame" had spoiled his life. The Mooni of the poem whose loss he laments is an imaginative ideal landscape of youthful innocence and joy. The protective, custodial nature of the landscape is highlighted by his wistful memories of the gifts it bestows. It makes its inmate a "shining sharer of that larger life," brings to his ears "psalms from unseen wildernesses," to his eyes gleams of "noonday dew in cool green grasses," to his soul respite from the world and "its sneers and spurning." He has lost all these — and the poem is filled "with his yearnings for them. It is in this backward look of regret for vanished innocence and joy that "Mooni" differs from the later "To a Mountain." "Mooni" seeks refuge in the untroubled past. "To a Mountain" has no such preoccupation with the peace that comes from evasion and flight.

The reason for the difference in attitude between the two poems es in the new awareness that had come to Kendall in the five years hat intervened. By 1880 he had learned that real peace comes with elf-knowledge and self-discipline. This was a conclusion that he had limpsed, years earlier, in "The Maid of Gerringong" and "Fainting y the Way," but the problems that swamped his life had driven that outhful wisdom from his mind. Kendall half-apologized to Ioldsworth for the unhappy air of the poem — "the verses are too ke Narrara . . . still I am confoundedly miserable." There is bitter elf-reproach as he speaks of his arrogant disregard of man and God n the thoughtless, self-centred years. In acknowledgement of his ;uilt "he shrinks before the splendid/Face of Deity offended" and iis punishment is that "all the loveliness is ended." Self-pity is still present. There is an implied rebuke against "certain hearts" that have ceased" to love him and commiseration with himself for the urt from which he claims he will never recover. "Mooni," with its ugubrious air, appeals to the same sentimental nostalgia as did 'Bell-Birds" and "September in Australia." It is cleverly con-tructed. The short lines, with their recurring rhymes (the same ound repeated for three consecutive lines) and the lingering, nostalgic emphasis created by the repetition of the first and last lines of the stanza, produce an hypnotic flow of sound that allows no dis-raction from the melancholy but balmy Mooni world:

> Ah, to be by Mooni now!
> Where the great dark hills of wonder,
> Scarred with storm and cleft asunder
> By the strong sword of the thunder,
> Make a night on morning's brow!
> Just to stand where Nature's face is
> Flushed with power in forest places —
> Where of God authentic trace is —
> Ah, to be by Mooni now!

The frequent rhymes tested Kendall's rather suspect ear. He made do with some poor approximations, for example, "face is, places," "abhorrent, current," "stress is, wildernesses," "river, ever." Weak lines and images are plentiful:

> And the streams of shadow hiss.

> Housed beneath the gracious kirtle
> Of the shadowy water-myrtle —
> Winds may hiss with heat and hurtle.

112

> Where the water-blossoms glister,
> And, by gleaming vale and vista
> Sits the English April's sister.

Popular though it has proved to be "Mooni" indicates no marked improvement in Kendall's lyric competence.

The two poems "Araluen" and "On a Street," both published in 1879, complete this purging of Kendall's conscience for the events of the years 1869-73. In "Araluen"[13] he makes his peace at last with the ghost of the baby girl who had haunted his memory for almost ten years. His guilt over her death had led to the hallucinations of 1872, when he imagined that he was accused of murdering a baby and to frequent dreams in which he met "the phantom of a wailing child." At the beginning of 1870, Kendall, broken by alcohol and poverty, had moved with his wife and child to a tiny cottage in Swan Street, Richmond, a poor Melbourne suburb. There on February 2, 1870, Araluen, thirteen months old, died of illness aggravated by malnutrition and was allegedly buried in a pauper's grave in an area of the Melbourne General Cemetery, known as "No Man's Land." The poem "Araluen" reveals nothing of the depressing ugliness of these actual events. It is a romanticized version of the baby's burial. She is laid to rest in a tranquil bush setting where sun and rain will "dress the spot with beauty" and where "blue-eyed Spring" will shower its bounty upon the tiny grave. This evasion of distressing reality ought not to be judged too harshly. Kendall's being had been revolted beyond endurance by the circumstances of the baby's death (as his breakdown in 1872 shows) and the imaginative gloss of this poem allowed him to express, for once, his love and grief rather than his guilty shame. The poem is equally concerned with the young mother who has lost her "first and sweetest" child. The reactions of the two people to each other beside that forlorn grave in Melbourne on the summer morning of 1870 will never be known, but Kendall's tender expression in "Araluen" of solicitude and love for his grieving wife must surely have healed whatever breach those sad days had caused between them. Although too sentimental for some tastes, "Araluen" is, for those who respond to it, one of Kendall's most moving and poignant personal poems.

"On a Street"[14] covers much the same biographical ground but without the concealment and disguise of "Araluen." It is a direct confession (later said by his wife to be somewhat exaggerated) of the cruelty that his drunkenness had inflicted on her — her furtive pawning of their linen and clothes for food, her search for pieces of wood for fuel to keep them warm, her shamed avoidance of friends and acquaintances. More sentimental even than "Araluen" the poem scarcely survives such melodramatic images as:

> A mother's curse is on the place.

> A lady in a faded print,
> A careworn writer for the Press.

> . . . the brutal curse
> Of landlord clamouring for his pay.

> The scholar on the taproom floor.

Occasionally the strength of the poet's feelings breaks the cloying hold of such phrases and gives a ring of emotional sincerity to the poem:

> A fierce old memory drags me back —
> I hate its name — I dread that street.
> . . . .
> How gladly would I change my theme,
> Or cease the song and steal away,
> But on the hill, and by the stream
> A ghost is with me night and day!
> . . . .
> But-still I hate that haggard street —
> Its filthy courts, its alleys wild!
> In dreams of it I always meet
> The phantom of a wailing child.

Kendall believed the poem to be among the best he had written. That estimate could have had nothing to do with its poetic qualities and can only have stemmed from his relief at having publicly admitted, and therefore exorcised, his guilt — an essential step in attaining the stability and peace of "To a Mountain."

The poems discussed, particularly the three "1872" poems, together with "Orara" (of 1879)[15] and "Names Upon a Stone,"[16] are the chief lyric poems of this last period. They have usually been accepted as superior to the landscape lyrics of *Leaves from Australian Forests,* but the reader who expects to find in them evidence of a new, much-improved lyrist will find that the difference is minimal. There are fewer occasions when sense and meaning are abandoned for sound effects and there is a deeper awareness of the natural scene and its impact on the human spirit. But there is the same obsession with inept and showy imagery ("the soft white feet of afternoon" of "Orara") and an even more pronounced tone of plaintive sentimentality and melancholy. If they are accepted as the best of Kendall's lyrics they can only reinforce the feeling that Kendall's literary talent did not lie in that genre.

III *Satirical Verse*

Nettled by persistent attacks from the writers of *Sydney Punch* Kendall made one early essay into satirical verse — "The Bronze Trumpet"[17] of 1865 — but it was not until late in his poetic life that he freely indulged his strong taste for this type of writing. In earlier years the caustic, sardonic side of his nature had occasionally been allowed expression in personal letters to friends but his public demeanor had normally been mild and unaggressive. In his final years however, he was quick to lampoon, in prose and verse, events which annoyed and people who displeased him, while old injustices and injuries, imagined or real, which had been dormant for years suddenly reemerged, provoking him into vicious attack.

IV *"The Bronze Trumpet"*

Sydney Punch, reestablished in 1864 after the failure of earlier versions in 1848, 1856 and 1857, drew its humorous and satirical material from many of the best-known writers of the day, writers such as Sheridan Moore, Deniehy, G. G. McCrae, Dalley, Barton, Garnet Walch and Kendall himself. Kendall's article, "About Some Men of Letters in Australia," shows that he was an active member of *Punch's* staff:

The contributors used to meet once a week, over cognac and cigars to think out a cartoon for the next issue, and to decide upon the character of the corresponding letterpress. On these occasions Dalley used to sit oozing wit and humour. Some of the happiest hits made by *Punch* were originally suggested by him; and his knack of concocting subjects for happy topical cartoons in the dullest of times was something remarkable . . . . At these pleasant *Punch* meetings of the past we were a Bohemian brotherhood![18]

This happy relationship apparently soured, for Kendall himself became the butt of *Punch's* satire. His poems have always proved easy to parody — witness Marcus Clarke's skit "Glycera" (and the verses in the *Bulletin* on April 9, 1881) which successfully aped the Kendall tone:

Glycera, my loved, my lost one, give me whiskey over proof,
In the moonless, mild mid-winters, when the rain is on the roof,
You that love, and you that listen, black in breaths of stormy traits,
Drift with me to death's division, driven by the fierce-aged fates;
This and this you have to reckon, when the wind on window beats,
And the little schoolboys trembling put their heads beneath the sheets.

Similar parodies of Kendall poems appeared in *Punch* in 1865, together with snide comments such as "The Glen of the Whiteman's Grave" being "the very blankest verse" and "Cui Bono?" being "a charming lyric of the particularly ridiculous and generally nonsensical school of which Mr. Kendall is undeniably facile princeps." In January, 1866, there appeared an anonymous pamphlet, "The Bronze Trumpet," dedicated to "the Shams Political, Clerical and Critical of Sydney and (in particular) to the Puny Punsters of Punch." Henry Halloran and Sheridan Moore were both suspected of having written it but most evidence, internal and external, points to Kendall's authorship. His comment to Harpur on December 2, 1865, is usually interpreted as referring to "The Bronze Trumpet": "I have written a satire upon some mock 'men of letters' which you will like I think. It is published in pamphlet form. If I haven't walked into Barton, Martin, Dalley etc. 'it's a caution' as the natives say."

"The Bronze Trumpet," a poem of more than 400 lines, contained numerous references to political, religious and literary figures of the day, most of whom are now obscure and unimportant. It begins with a conversation between the English and Australian sister Muses, the "Muse of Albion" self-assured and arrogant, "Urania of the South" diffident and introverted. The English Muse fashioned a peculiarly English musical instrument, "a broadmouthed trumpet," which she intended Australian bards to use. Kendall criticizes here the English influence on the shaping of newly born Australian song. The "Muse of Albion" offered the trumpet to her Australian sister to pass on to the Australian poet most fitted to "shape for other days a Song divine." The shy Muse made hesitant suggestions — Harpur, Kendall, Barton, Dalley. All were discarded by the English maiden. In this discussion Kendall was able to insert a good word for Harpur and himself, and direct a few jibes at Barton and Dalley:

116   HENRY KENDALL

    . . . Her Austral sister turned
    With lips that faltered, but with heart that burned,
    And answered humbly: "May my Harpur try —
    "My first-born, wedded to weird Ecstasy?"
    "No — no!" she cried, "let Harpur keep his ease
    "Amongst his native streams and rocks and trees;
    "He'd dabble in aesthetics, and I know
    "My work is not for Harpur — let him go!"
    Then asked the other: "Shall young Kendall rise?
    "His wings are used to travelling through the skies?
    "Behold of late he took a flight afar
    "And sped like comet, out from star to star,
    "With furious tumult! Radiant Queen of mine,
    "Shall Kendall rise and take the flight divine?"
    To whom the Maiden, in a lower tone:
    "My task is not for pinions barely grown"
    I've thought of him; and then of one who weeps,
    "A tuneful Poet, where Ione sleeps,
    "He *hath* the strength; but we must even leave
    "The spot where Love and pallid Memory grieve."
    Then cried once more the sister hopefully —
    "I've hit the chosen — shall brisk Barton try?
    "That *bearded bard* — the prince of scented swells?"
    "*He,* sister! why he wears a jester's bells!"
    "Shall brilliant Dalley to the honour pass?
    "He rides a Pegasus!" — "He rides an ass!"

Since no one was deemed worthy, the Australian Muse took the trumpet herself and "startled Sydney" with her song.

In the "Song" Kendall began an immediate attack. The first "blast" of the trumpet was for Judge H. R. Francis who had offended Kendall in a public lecture early in 1865:

    . . . Let our Francis grace
    His petty audience with his nightly face;
    Yea, let him twist his mouth, and snarl and sneer,
    On bench and platform, yelping year by year!
    What though the *Herald* dubs his lectures 'treats',
    Those changeless dishes of familiar meats.
    Are they the newer? Will they tickle more
    Because we've had them fifty times before?

The attack continued on colonial critics in general and G. B. Barton in particular. Barton, the author in 1866 of *The Poets and Prose*

Writers of New South Wales and *Literature in New South Wales*,
was one whom Kendall felt was malicious rather than constructive:

> But sing, my Poets! While brisk Barton bites
> His wretched pen and writes, as now he writes
> For very malice, wherefore curb your verse?
> Than *his*, remember, it can be no worse!
> Yea, sing away, although the criticlings,
> Like full-grown critics, are for clipping wings;
> And though young Pegasus doth feel the flies
> That round his haunches rise and fall and rise,
> And cannot whisk aside the tedious bunch
> From surly S-dd-n down to snivelling *Punch*.

His attack grew more virulent and personal. The churchman, Rev.
W. H. H. Yarrington (Mawworm) was described in bitingly fluent
couplets as

> . . . the mild epitome
> Of all a well-bred flunkey ought to be?
> A sleek-cut rascal of the ranting race
> Who cannot look his Bishop in the face?

His chief target among the *Punch* writers was Derwent Coleridge
(Dibbler) whom he saw as the instigator of most of the attacks on
him. He named others and bellowed defiance at them.

> Come, gentle Dibbler! candid critic dear
> With sidelong eye and thin perpetual sneer!
> *Thou* hast thy fond disciples; *they* remain
> Bound like to faithful watchdogs on thy chain;
> *They'll* bark at those who threat! With *thee* to lead,
> They'll follow and be like to *dogs* indeed!
> . . . .
> "Cry out, 'no mercy!' slip you line and leash,
> Buchanan, Lucas, Cummings, Rodd, Dalgleish!
> *Et ceteri*, if you like, come great — come small —
> I have no terror — here is '*at you all!*'
> I shall not step aside, or sag with fear
> For you, ye foxes, whining in my rear!

The procession of names and offences continued. Some references
are vague and uninteresting, but the attack is saved from tedium by

the outbursts of blunt condemnation and sudden sallies of wit. Of his irritators in general he said: "I fain would know how much the mongrels dare,/Who bark in kennels, in the open air." Of one in particular:

> Some churls have whispered, (let me say it low)
> That thou art, after all, a sorry foe —
> That 'heavy vanity and heavy lead
> Fill up the crannies' of thy 'ponderous head'!
> But *I* — I don't believe it! I have tried
> And found — nor lead nor anything beside!

Colonial newspapers were criticized for their hotch-potch of "Aesthetics, Venus, Cricket, Poetry" and for their reliance on "pointless pun and slanderous joke." With most of his venom spent Kendall came to the point of the poem, the attacks on his work. The anonymity of the poem allowed him to make his assessment of himself without embarrassment. The melancholy, self-indulgent tone betrays Kendall's authorship as plainly as does the familiar ring of a line such as "swift water-moons blown into golden lights":

"You're hard on Kendall, caustic critics . . .
He *too* has been a dreamer, though you damn
His many efforts and baptize him 'sham':
Once, in his 'springtime', when his heart was soft,
He *too* could rhyme by stream and field and croft;
And, as a traveller sees in windy nights
Swift water-moons blown into golden lights,
You might have seen across his face of yore
The swift delights of thoughts that are no more!
But these are dead, and, like a wearied guest,
He has *few* thoughts now past the thought of rest —
Few thoughts, my masters: not through you and yours,
But through a sorrow no man well endures.
Yea, steeped in trouble to the very lip,
He stands and fronts you like a lonely ship
That strives with all the sea — well beaten down
By winds that buffet and by rains that drown.

For various reasons — the doubt over its authorship, the decline in popularity of formal satire, the lack of interest in the petty squabbles that inspired it — "The Bronze Trumpet" has attracted little interest down the years. It shows, however, that satire came easily to Kendall. His quick intelligence and sure eye for the ridiculous (in others rather than himself) was combined with a streak of vindictiveness that spurred him into sudden and violent criticism. He was capable of coarse abusive insults, stinging sarcasm, and spiteful innuendo — all of which are present in "The Bronze Trumpet." But there is also evidence in the poem of deft satirical technique. This is particularly noticeable in his easy, fluent handling of the heroic couplet and the resultant, rather pleasing, epigrammatic quality that clings to the lines. This terse conciseness lends to his barbs that essential characteristic of satire, the assumption that the attack is unanswerable, that riposte is useless.

After "The Bronze Trumpet" there was no further satirical outburst until the late 1870s when he began to write a series of skits and lampoons, especially for the *Freeman's Journal* and the *Town and Country Journal*. These satirical verses paid well and seemed to please him. They served, perhaps, as an outlet for some of the frustrations that had built up over the years and he may have gained pleasure from handing out a little criticism instead of receiving it. The later poems confirm his obvious talent for this type of writing, whether it was sophisticated and formal satire or mere mudslinging.

V "*The Gagging Bill*"

The best of Kendall's political satires is "The Gagging Bill," [19] published in the *Freeman's Journal* June 7, 1879. Kendall became involved in the furore over the controversial Parliamentary Powers and Privileges Bill of 1878 when Thomas Butler, the *Freeman's* editor, requested some verses lampooning it. The Bill carried penal clauses which could be used against persons who criticized members of Parliament, such criticism being interpreted as a breach of Parliamentary privilege. Most people who opposed the Bill saw it as an attempted curb on the freedom of speech, especially freedom of the Press. Though passed by the lower House, it was opposed and amended in the upper House and after long, bitter argument throughout 1878 - 79 finally thrown out altogether.

Kendall's poem was hastily written — in four hours according to his own report — and was sent off without reconsideration of its contents or tone. Although he was persuaded later into expressing some regret for the attack on Sir Henry Parkes, Kendall, in the exhilaration of the moment, fancied himself only as the outspoken defender of public liberty. To Peter Fagan he wrote: "The tone is severe; but my feelings were considerably excited over this gross attempt to gag the mouth of public opinion."[20] He gave Henry Halloran a more detailed justification of his action as well as an interesting and frank assessment of his relationship with Parkes:

For many years past, I have never written a line for or against Sir Henry Parkes. I could not praise the body of his actions as a public man, because I did not care to lie, and I could not condemn him because I felt fettered by the bonds of obligation. But that last act of his, that gross attempt to gag the mouth of public opinion has been too much for me. A satire appearing in this week's *Freeman* is the issue of a feeling that has quite overpowered personal friendship. Like Brutus however I do not love Caesar less because I love Rome more. Parkes has done many noble beautiful things; he is a man of immense capacity but with absolute power in his hands, he would become a very bloody edition of Draco. In high places he loses balance.[21]

After an initial burst of abuse against Stephen Brown, lawyer and politician with whom he was at loggerheads over certain educational proposals (Brown was a member of the New South Wales Council of Education), Kendall parades the great names in Australia's struggle for freedom and independence — Wentworth, Lowe, Bland, Forbes, Windeyer — and contrasts them with the present Parliamentary representatives, one a "butcher with the faithless face," another "an ass . . . that sets its ears and brays," none of them fit men "to lift the State and shape the best decrees." But this is merely the introduction to his vitriolic attack on Parkes. For almost fifty lines he engages in one of the most scornful, insulting and devastating onslaughts on an eminent public figure that Australian literature contains:

> O hide for shame, ye foolish ones, and blind,
> Who made a ruler of a bag of wind!
> Who placed your freedom in the reach of sharks,
> And fell from Pericles to — Henry Parkes!
> Great statesman this! the upstart of a day
> To dare to say what Bismarck would not say!
> Pure patriot he who, with his motley crew,
> Was fain to do what Draco would not do!
>
> . . . .
> Is this your model ruler? — turn and shout,
> Ye boobies, while I trot your idol out!
> Here is the man . . .
> Who crept to power in his peculiar mode
> And stuck at nothing on the nasty road —

Who ran with every wind, and gained his ends
By buying foes and sacrificing friends!
. . . .
Lo, here is he who tried to set his foot
On Freedom's flower and crush it leaf and root!
Who made a wild attempt to overreach
And kill that right august — our right of speech!
. . . .
A wretched flunkey in a 'ducal' dress —
He bridle Liberty — *he* gag the Press!
He put it out — the fine imperial flame,
And make an English-speaking people tame!
A thing like him — a mushroom of the mire —
Is he the one to cope with lordly-fire?

In spite of its half-truths and exaggerations this is a magnificent
piece of satirical declamation. It is full of the theatrical devices so
vital to impassioned rhetoric — shrivelling contempt to bludgeon his
audience into cowed submission; explosive sarcasm and deflatory
ridicule to demolish his enemy; derisive questions and inflammatory
taunts. All this with a gusto and verve impossible to be denied, with
a blazing arrogance that dismisses opposition before it forms. But it
"overreaches." Technically superb as it is it fails ultimately because
Kendall loses control, not of his rhetoric, for that copes beautifully
with the buildup of vituperation, but of the quality of conviction in
what he has to say. There were many people who might have
believed that Parkes was intent on filching their freedoms, that he
did use ruthless political skullduggery in his climb to power. Faults
such as these had at least the grace of magnitude — and one would
expect the nation's leader, if he were evil, to be evil on a grand scale.
But when Kendall allowed his private spleen to show — "a wretched
flunkey," "a mushroom of the mire" — his lofty public attack
dropped away into ugly, ineffective, personal spite.

"The Gagging Bill" drew considerable wrath upon Kendall's
obstinately unrepentant head. Parkes was, naturally, offended and
Halloran pressed Kendall to apologize. In a letter to Parkes he
defended his principles but failed to account for the personal
animosity of the poem: "I have never been disloyal to the friend who
placed me under so many obligations in the sorrowful dead years.
We are not boys; and you know very well that a man like me is likely
to champion his political convictions at all risks and under all cir-

cumstances. For my attacks on certain features of your policy, I offer
no apology and feel no remorse."[22]

The final section of "The Gagging Bill" praises W. B. Dalley, who
had led the opposition to the legislation, as lavishly as the earlier
lines had damned Parkes. Once directed to eulogy the poem fades
away into stereotyped paeans of praise which are pale and uninteresting compared with the furious satire of the attack on Parkes.

Parkes was also the butt of "The Sawyer Who Works on the
Top"[23] (like "The Gagging Bill," strangely excluded from Reed's
The Poetical Works of Henry Kendall). It was published in the
Freeman's Journal, August 30, 1879, less than two months after
"The Gagging Bill." Using the fact that Parkes had been, before
emigrating, the owner of a Birmingham business, Kendall attaches
to him the tag "Brummagen," an opprobrious nickname for poor
quality Birmingham goods. There is nothing meritorious in this second poem; it is merely a succession of crude insults strung together
on the argument that Parkes shows no talent as a politician, that he is
a "charlatan" and should be thrown out. The analogy is made with a
skilled tradesman such as a sawyer, who, unlike Parkes, if he does not
know his job fails to get one. The title is ingenious but the remainder
of the satire is unimaginative and clumsy, with personal insults plentiful. Parkes is "gigantic in limb and in paw," "only a barrel of talk"
and "a doll of old women and fools." The lusty contempt of "The
Gagging Bill's" "Is this your model ruler? — turn and shout,/Ye
boobies, while I trot your idol out" gives way to contrived, in-
nocuous, indirect aspersions:

> Is he fit for his eminent post?
> Does he know how to "sharpen" and "set"?
> In spite of his swagger and boast
> You know he is Brummagen yet.

In spite of his protestations that there was nothing personal in all
these attacks Kendall's animus against Parkes seems to have been
nurtured by years of brooding. He had relied on Parkes for
patronage in the early days, and Parkes usually obliged. But Kendall
felt, and was probably made to feel, his dependent status. He
received, on one occasion, a lukewarm response to his request for
promotion into Parkes's Colonial Secretary's Office and felt belittled
by the situation. "I cannot help thinking you were on the occasion of
my last visit not as you have been with me. I have never been a

parasite," Kendall wrote.[24] When he was in absolute poverty in Melbourne, Parkes pressed him for payment of an old debt. Kendall replied: "Long before I had a thought of throwing up my situation your manner to me became painfully frigid. It repelled and silenced me. . . . I left Sydney with no more prominent desire in my mind than to meet your loan and meet it quickly. . . . As to your threat to commence legal proceedings against me such a course of action would merely complete my ruin."[25] From 1868 to 1872 Kendall alienated all but a few close friends with his wayward behaviour and his irresponsible attitude towards borrowing and repaying money. When retribution came with his breakdown in 1872 he was inclined to blame everyone but himself. Parkes and others (his wife, and Marcus Clarke in Melbourne) became associated in his mind with those disastrous times and unhappily they had to bear the brunt of his hostility for their imagined transgressions.

VI *"The Song of Ninian Melville"*

The satire[26] which Dalley warned William Maddock might become the centre of a *cause célèbre* was also aimed at a political figure. Ninian Melville, born in Sydney, 1843, was at first a cabinet maker ("the coffin biz"), then became active in local government, being at one time Mayor of Newtown, an inner Sydney suburb. His election as Member of Parliament for Northumberland led to Kendall's tirade against him. The detailing of Melville's activities in the poem indicates Kendall's personal awareness of every stage of his career. Melville is accused of being a rabble-rouser — a stirrer of political, industrial, religious and racial strife:

In the fly-blown village pothouse, where a dribbling bag of beer,
Passes for a human being, Nin commenced his new career —
Talked about the "Christian swindle" — cut the Bible into bits —
Shook his fist at Mark and Matthew — gave the twelve Apostles fits:
Slipped into the priests and parsons — hammered at the British Court —
Boozy boobies were astonished: lubbers of the Lambton sort!
Yards of ear were cocked to listen — yards of mouth began to shout,
'Here's a cove as is long-headed — Ninny knows his way about!'

So it came to pass that Melville — *Mister* Melville, I should say —
Dodged about with deputations, half a dozen times a day!
Started strikes and bossed the strikers — damned employers, every one,
On the Column — off the Column — in the shanty — in the sun!
'Down with masters — up with wages! keep the 'pigtail' out of this!'

This is what our Ninny shouted — game you see, of hit or miss!
World, of course, is full of noodles — some who bray at Wallsend sent
Thing we know to be a windbag bouncing into Parliament!

Melville is accused of contempt for the working man, "soaping down
the ''orny-'anded' is the safest 'bizness' out!" Kendall is as disgusted
with the working man as he is with Melville. His picture of the
worker is an indictment of the lower-class male but, as usual with
such accusations, it is too sweeping to be just. Yet there is an element
of uncomfortable truth in it:

> . . . by Jove, I'd like to tan
> Back of that immense impostor that they call the "working man"!
> Drag upon our just employers — sponger on a worn-out wife —
> Boozing in some alley pothouse every evening of his life!
> Type he is of Nin's supporters: tot him up and tot him down,
> He would back old Nick tomorrow for the sake of half a crown

The final verse deplores the sacrilege of Melville's presence in the
". . . Chamber where the voice of Lowe/And the lordly words of
Wentworth sounded thirty years ago." The poem is scurrilous
abuse from beginning to end and apart from the few copies that es-
caped Maddock's roundup it was not published. Whether Melville
contemplated action is now difficult to say but in a little over eighteen months Kendall was dead and there the matter ended. The
poem arouses interest now only because of its unusual history. Its
literary value is nonexistent. The emphatic rise and fall of the lines is
similar to an exaggerated version of the old fifteenth-century "paus-
ing metre" and this gives the rollicking, songlike effect which the title implies. Flippant, slangy colloquialisms are in almost every line
but they are clearly deliberate. Kendall no doubt feeling that this
was the proper level of language in which Melville should be
described. The verses are a good example of the "newspaper" satire
which found favor with readers of the day.

VII "Bill the Bullock Driver" and "Jim the Splitter"

These two poems, among the earliest attempts to depict
Australian bush characters in the style later popularized by the bush
balladists, are usually accepted as good-natured raillery rather than
deliberate satire; yet Kendall's critical intent is obvious in them. The
tone of the bush ballad is usually ironic, the central figures, outback

personalities such as shearers, drovers, teamsters, rousabouts, being portrayed in mock-heroic terms which, while applauding their sturdy independence, ingenuity, amiability and laconic, easy-going nature, also underline their narrow-minded parochialism, gaucherie, insensitivity and scallywaggery. Kendall captures the ambivalent nature of his two subjects remarkably well.

"Bill the Bullock Driver"[27] was published in 1876 in the *Town and Country Journal* and "Jim the Splitter"[28] in the *Freeman's Journal* in 1880. In submitting "Jim" to Thomas Butler, editor of the *Freeman*, Kendall added a note of explanation for his rough handling of the character:

"Jim the Splitter" is my latest effort in the metrical line [the ballad metre?]. I have headed it with my real name because I like it. Its chief merit lies in its truth. No doubt it is rough on the "orny-'anded" but your bushman is one of the most finished rogues out. I ought to know having had such an unhappy business connection with him. The "Heathen Chinee" [accepted as the outback's most adept "fleecer"] is a child to the beggar. My poem will "take" with a large class of sufferers.[29]

Jim's lack of culture is the subject of the opening verses. The irony is doubly directed — at Jim who is "poetical rarely" and at the arid intellectuality of much classical and literary knowledge. Jim has his own brand of "bush" knowledge which serves his purpose better than an acquaintance with Euripides, Homer, "Ruskin, Rossetti or Dante":

> His knowledge is this — he can tell in the dark
> What timber will split, by the feel of the bark;
> And, rough as his manner of speech is,
> His wits to the fore he can readily bring
> In passing off ash as the genuine thing,
> When scarce in the forest the beech is.
>
> In "girthing" a tree that he sells "in the round",
> He assumes as a rule that its body is sound,
> And measures — *forgetting to bark it!*
> He may be a ninny; but still the old dog
> Can plug to perfection the pipe of a log
> And "palm it" away on the market.
>
> He splits a fair shingle; but holds to the rule
> Of his father's, and haply his grandfather's school —

126

HENRY KENDALL

> Which means that he never has blundered,
> When tying his shingles, by slinging in more
> Than the recognized number of ninety and four,
> To the bundle he sells for a hundred.

Although exposing and lightly satirizing such sharp practices Kendall goes on to indicate his admiration for Jim's mastery of his own particular art of shingle splitting. Australian appreciation of the utilitarian has always been greater than its appreciation of the cultural. In the bush ballads there is usually open ridicule of the effete aestheticism of sophisticated society and applause for the practical capacity and adaptability of "bush" people. Kendall was the product of both societies — he admired Jim's ability as sawyer and splitter but was irritated by the bushman's habit of believing that this limited excellence betokened superiority over the world at large. His comments on this attitude are suitably tart:

> He shines at his best at the tiller of saw,
> On the top of the pit, where his whisper is law
> To the gentleman working below him.
> When the pair of them pause in a circle of dust,
> Like a monarch he *poses* exalted, august —
> There's nothing this planet can show him!

> For a man is a *man* who can "sharpen" and "set";
> And *he* is the only thing masculine yet.

In a similar poem, "Billy Vicars,"[30] written also in 1880, Kendall directly attacks this quality of ignorant boastfulness in a certain outback type. Billy Vicars was a prime example of the loudmouthed know-it-all, who, because of his limited imagination and sheer insensitivity (though he had ample natural cunning) was able to survive and prosper in an environment which might have destroyed more gentle souls.

In "Bill the Bullock Driver" the isolated, circumscribed bushman's world, the world of Lawson's "hasn't any opinions, hasn't any idears,"[31] illustrates the narrowness of the outback life and its people.

> The leaders of millions — the lords of the lands
> Who sway the wide world with their will,
> And shake the great globe with the strength of their hands,

Flash past us — unnoticed by Bill.
. . . .
The singers that sweeten all time with their songs —
Pure voices that make us forget
Humanity's drama of marvellous wrong,
To Bill are as mysteries yet.

In describing the simple, uncomplicated life of the teamster his tone is affectionate and kindly, but his praise for the ingenuous, open-hearted Bill is partly tongue-in-cheek. Although mostly ignored by popular opinion, there are satirical echoes in the well-known "school room" lines:

> As straight and as sound as a slab without crack,
> Our Bill is a king in his way:
> Though he camps by the side of a shingle track,
> And sleeps on the bed of his dray.
>
> A whiplash to him is as dear as a rose
> Would be to a delicate maid:
> He carries his darlings wherever he goes
> In a pocket-book tattered and frayed.
>
> The joy of a bard when he happens to write
> A song like the song of his dream
> Is nothing at all to our hero's delight
> In the pluck and the strength of his team.
>
> For the kings of the earth — for the faces august
> Of princes, the millions may shout:
> To Bill as he lumbers along in the dust,
> A bullock's the grandest thing out.

Poets have generally pictured the bushman as oblivious to the natural glory that surrounds him. Some, like Lawson, have tended to picture the countryside as devoid of beauty anyway, a merciless terrain of blazing deserts, scorching plains and flooded rivers. To them it is an enemy to be defeated not a beauty to be wooed and loved. Kendall's deepest indictment of the "bullocky" is his insensitivity to the loveliness of the countryside through which he plods, and his pragmatic evaluation of its natural riches:

> To the mighty, magnificent temples of God
> In the hearts of the dominant hills

Bill's eyes are as blind as the fire-blackened clod
That burns far away from the rills.

Through beautiful bountiful forests that screen
A marvel of blossoms from heat —
Whose lights are the mellow and golden, and green —
Bill walks with irreverent feet.

The manifold splendours of mountain and wood
By Bill like nonentities slip:
He loves the black myrtle because it is good
As a handle to lash to his whip.

In his adept handling of the ballad meter Kendall demonstrated, yet again, the versatility of his poetic talent. The difference between his two poems and the later bush ballads lies in the more elevated "poetic" language (a typical colonial mannerism) which breaks through in spite of his effort to keep the tone deliberately casual and in his somewhat embarrassed attitude (similarly colonial) to the cultural shortcomings of his "heroes." The nationalist writers nearer the end of the century reflected the change in outlook of the new generation by accepting the absence of gentility and polish as a laudable sign of "Australian" character.

VIII *The International Exhibition Verses*

The International Exhibitions held in consecutive years in Sydney, 1879, and Melbourne, 1880, were saluted with specially composed verse and song. Kendall had been commissioned to write opening and closing cantatas for the Sydney event and he also submitted the winning entry in the *Sydney Morning Herald's* poetry competition held in conjunction with it.

The prize poem, originally entitled "Australia,"[32] was about 300 lines in length. Within days of its publication in the *Herald* it had sparked a controversy, some critics disliking its complexity and innovatory language. Ironically, it was *Sydney Punch* which defended Kendall against these objections. The judges of the competition had sought a poem suitably appropriate to the occasion as well as possessing a high standard "of poetic thought and expression." Kendall's "Australia" was successful from a field of 250 entries, a number of which were from England and America.

The opening lines call Calliope's attention (she was the Muse of epic poetry) to the remarkable natural beauty of Australia, beauty

which the poet hopes will persuade Calliope to lend her inspiration
to his song. He seeks from her "one hour/Of life pre-eminent with
perfect power" that he may fashion, for this lovely land and this particular occasion, an inspiring song. The poem then focuses on
Sydney, "the shining City of a hundred spires," in its gala dress of
"all the flags of all the World" for the International Exhibition. Kendall traces the discovery and settlement of the land, events which
brought it out of its legendary mystery, where "old fallacious tales"
believed it wrapped in polar darkness or "chained down with ice and
ringed with sleepless gales." He recalls the first unknown French
voyages, then the Dutch landings on the Carpentaria coast in 1605
when "Strong sons of Europe, in a far dim year,/Faced ghastly foes
and felt the alien spear!" Hartog and Tasman make way for Dam-
pier and the first "clear bold sounds of English speech," then Cap-
tain Cook, "the daring son of gray old Yorkshire," who on a gentle
Autumn day in April first beheld "the bay of flowers," Botany Bay.
With the arrival of Phillip and the First Fleet "this land's majestic
Yesterday/Of immemorial silence died away." The Australian scene
of that summer ninety years earlier is visualized in couplets of
strong, imaginative impact:

> Where are the woods that, ninety summers back,
> Stood hoar with ages by the water-track?
> Where are the valleys of the flashing wing,
> The dim green margins, and the glimmering spring?
> Where now the warrior of the forest race,
> His glaring war-paint and his fearless face?

The natural beauty has been devastated; woods and valleys
despoiled by ax and plough; birds and animals driven by fear into
faraway hiding places in the hills. Of the tribes all that remains is "A
shadowy relic in a mountain cave,/A ghost of fire in immemorial
hills." But the nineteenth century was the age of "progress" and
such events as the International Exhibition were created specifically
for man to admire his busy ingenuity and to worship the fruits of his
labor. Predictably Kendall's poem focuses on the benefits which the
white man has brought — civilization. A symbol of this is the glory
of the city, spread out before his gaze. He praises the sturdy efforts
of those who built it from the wilderness:

> The human hands of strong, heroic men
> Broke down the mountain, filled the gaping glen,

> Ran streets through swamp, built banks against the foam,
> And bent the arch and raised the lordly dome!
> . . . .
> Here sleep the grand old men whose lives sublime
> Of thought and action shine and sound through time!
> Who worked in darkness — onward fought their ways
> To bring about these large majestic days —
> Who left their sons the hearts and high desires
> Which built this City of the hundred spires.

The brightest feature to meet his eyes is the opulent Garden Palace, the "miracle of dome and minaret," within whose walls the countries of the world gathered their achievements of "dazzling Science" and Art. By hosting this celebration of man's achievements Kendall believes that Australia increases her own stature. The moment of this Exhibition marks her maturity. Henceforth "her place will be with mighty lords." The poem ends with suitably conventional praise to God for His bounty and hopes that His benevolence will shine upon the land.

The lack of critical interest in Kendall's "Exhibition" poem is unfortunate for it contains some of his best poetry and still further emphasizes his remarkable poetic range. In Kendall's day interest in public poetry, especially when set in the formal pattern of Augustan verse with its eternal round of couplets and its elevated, impersonal tone, had largely disappeared. Contemporary critics, forced to concede that such a prominent occasion still required the customary celebratory ode, scarcely felt called upon to enthuse about the poem itself which they felt was bound to be merely eulogy by prescription. They were wrong in their dismissal of it. It is a sincerely personal poem of praise for Australia. Kendall, the "Native Australian Poet" still, saw in the occasion an opportunity to express again his hopes for the future of the nation and his joy in its beauty and achievements. There is true patriotic pride in his vision:

> From hence, the morning beauty of her name
> Will shine afar, like an exceeding flame.
> Her place will be with mighty lords, whose sway
> Controls the thunder and the marching day:
> Her crown will shine beside the crowns of kings
> Who shape the seasons, rule the course of things.
> The fame of her across the years to be

> Will spread like light on a surpassing sea;
> And graced with glory, girt with power august,
> Her life will last till all things turn to dust.

Readers persistently disappointed with Kendall's lyricism will find here indications of truer lyric grace. There are still the old Kendall faults — elegant-sounding but empty phrases such as "dells of peace and plenilune," "waters dear to days of blue" — and the irritating repetition of the archaic, awkward, poetic construction "What time" instead of the simple "when" in lines such as

> What time he steered towards the southern snow.

> What time a gentle April shed its showers.

> What time the mists of morning westward rolled.

But there are many couplets that make a pleasing impression with their apt and attractive imagery:

> These are the coasts that old fallacious tales
> Chained down with ice and ringed with sleepless gales!

> In dreams of her he roved from zone to zone,
> And gave her lovely name to coasts unknown.

> The single savage yelling on the beach
> The dark strange curses of barbaric speech.

Throughout the poem description and comment blend, with some few exceptions, in a disciplined balance. There is still the typically attractive Kendall language, but it is not as feverishly exotic as in earlier days and it flows smoothly under unusual control. The whole poem has an air of mature composure that indicates the poet's confidence in his theme and in his capacity to treat that theme with sincerity and skill. With all this said it is easy to understand readers, of that day and this, turning away from the poem with only the briefest of glances. The formal ode of eulogy, significant as it has been in the overall history of literature, has a long record of unappealing artificiality. Kendall's poem has been a victim of the general distaste for this genre, which for the past century has been almost extinct and is likely to remain so.

IX *"The Verge of Aidenn"*

The dedicatory poem of this final volume, "To a Mountain,"[33] was the last poem of personal revelation written by Kendall and as such is a fitting poem with which to conclude this analysis of his work. It reveals the new Kendall, within reach of the mental and spiritual peace toward which the catharsis of the "Shadow of 1872" poems had been leading him. Years earlier in "Fainting by the Way" Kendall had indicated that the paradise of "Aidenn" did not have to be an imaginary state of bliss, attained only in another life. "Aidenn" could be gained in the composure and certainty that comes with self-knowledge and self-discipline. In this final poem he is clearly, at last, on "the verge of Aidenn."

"To a Mountain" has been acknowledged as one of his most impressive utterances. Judith Wright judges it his most significant poem:

. . . we may see this poem as including and transcending all Kendall's former poetic world — the dead poet he had once hailed as his 'Chief' [she detects a similar reverence for Harpur in Kendall's early poems as for the mountain in this poem], the 'tracts of burning desert' where he had stumbled with his explorers, the rivers of his lost childhood and their unattainable sources, the Christianity that had not greatly helped him; the Wordsworthianism (Harpur's originally) that is here so curiously mixed with it . . . , and finally Kendall's own Dream of an unattainable poetry and his final offering, his 'book of rhymes'. We are right to feel that this is Kendall's most significant poem; it is the poem in which he attains to self-understanding and thereby to his proper manhood.[34]

A. D. Hope is equally impressed.

It is a beautiful and elevated invocation, in plain and moving language, Kendall's profession of faith and his central vision of the world he celebrates. . . . It is a noble and sustained music which, whatever it may owe to Wordsworth and Tennyson, is Kendall's own voice. Had he been an English poet writing in England it would have won him a recognition sometimes denied or grudgingly bestowed by critics who would like it to include a few gum trees, bungalows, woolly-butts to guarantee that it is a genuine Australian product.[35]

More than most men Kendall needed to draw on a source of strength outside himself to sustain him though troubled periods. Throughout his life he had found this prop in many forms; in the young man's vision of a future paradise, in the romantic's belief in an ideal love, in the poet's confident hope of recognition, in the nature lover's dependence on the beauty and strength of beloved landscapes. When Kendall was deprived of these supports — as in the "Shadow of 1872" — his own strength was inadequate. His recovery after 1874 was partly due to the return of his props — his friendship with the Fagans, the restorative effect of the lovely Brisbane Water landscape, the renewed desire to write, his reunion with his wife and family. But there was a new and quite different attitude within himself. Older, and much wiser, he had finally gained some of the certainty and self-possession that he had lacked in earlier years. The dedicatory poem, "To a Mountain" explains this changed attitude. He sees the Mountain, Nature's own symbol of strength and stability, as a model upon which to build his new mature life; and he accepts the sadness of the past — "strong authentic sorrow" — with a newly acquired tranquility. This new calmness of spirit he attributes to the mountain. A symbolic, rather than actual, Mountain it is personified as a beloved father or teacher and addressed in tones of affectionate reverence. In dedicating the new volume to it Kendall does so with the belief that, if, within the book,

> There lives and glows *one* verse in which there beats
> The pulse of wind and torrent — if *one* line
> Is here that like a running water sounds,
> And seems an echo from the land of leaf,
> Be sure that line is thine.

Kendall shares, in the poem, Wordsworth's unusual type of pantheistic experience. Wordsworth believed, in "Tintern Abbey," that the Spirit

> Whose dwelling is the light of setting suns,
> And the round ocean and the living air
> . . . rolls through all things.

Kendall, too, believes that in Nature is "God's grand authentic gospel." From the Mountain, which he sees as a living, personal presence, he learns of "the higher worship . . . the larger faith." Kendall's religious feelings were not known to be unduly deep or earnest, most of his private or public comments being suitably conventional. These lines, however, carry an unusual emotional and

religious fervor — a fervor, which like Wordsworth's, appears to lead
him through Nature to God:

> . . . . Here in this home
> Away from men and books and all the schools,
> I take thee for my Teacher. In thy voice
> Of deathless majesty, I, kneeling, hear
> God's grand authentic gospel! Year by year
> The great sublime cantata of thy storm
> Strikes through my spirit — fills it with a life
> Of startling beauty! Thou my Bible art
> With holy leaves of rock, and flower, and tree,
> And moss, and shining runnel. From each page
> That helps to make thy awful Volume, I
> Have learned a noble lesson. In the psalm
> Of thy grave winds, and in the liturgy
> Of singing waters, lo! my soul has heard
> The higher worship; and from thee indeed
> The broad foundations of a finer hope
> Were gathered in; and thou has lifted up
> The blind horizon for a larger faith!

In the Kendall of earlier years there had sometimes been an
attempt to evade problems (the yearning for "Aidenn") or a flood
of self-pity because of them (the complaint of "the life austere").
"To a Mountain" recognizes, at last, the beneficent effect of a
manful shouldering of the burdens of life. Acceptance of one's
sorrows ". . . makes a man more human, and his life/More like that
frank exalted life of thine." The "life of thine" is that of the Mountain
and its stately, calm existence becomes his inspiration. The poem
concludes with fervent tributes to its remote steadfastness, its invul-
nerability to time and upheaval. The sea, the fountain, the wind, the
morning light — in essence, all Nature — is linked to it in magnificent immutability:

> . . . Round thy lordly capes the sea
> Rolls on with a superb indifference
> For ever; in thy deep green gracious glens
> The silver fountains sing for ever. Far
> Above dim ghosts of waters in the caves,
> The royal robe of morning on thy head
> Abides for ever! evermore the wind
> Is thy august companion: and thy peers

> Are cloud, and thunder, and the face sublime
> Of blue midheaven!

Its ultimate link is with God:

> . . . On thy awful brow
> Is Deity; and in that voice of thine
> There is the great imperial utterance
> Of God forever.

The poem suggests, as do others of these last years, that Kendall, through the landscape that he had loved so long and so well, had come to a new religious awareness. Through the Mountain it seems that he had come to peace with God. If this is true then it goes a long way towards explaining the peace that he seems finally to have come to with himself.

CHAPTER 5

Kendall's Prose Writing

K ENDALL began to write regularly for newspapers and journals when he needed money desperately in the years 1869 to
1873. There had been earlier spasmodic prose contributions such as
"Courtesy," published in the *Empire,* December 28, 1866, and
"Talkers," which appeared in the *Colonial Monthly Magazine,*
November, 1867; but the first regular flow of articles came in the
Australasian soon after his arrival in Melbourne in April, 1869. Many
of the *Australasian* articles, such as "Camped by a Snake" (May 15,
1869), "A Fight with a Devil Fish" (June 5, 1869), "Ghost Glen"
(June 26, 1869), "The Great Clarence River Flood" (April 2, 1870)
and "A Cruise Among the South Sea Islands" (May 7, 1870), are im-
aginative, descriptive anecdotes, aimed only at the light taste of
newspaper readers. He managed to have several literary articles
published in the *Australasian* during the same period, for example,
"The Holy Grail" (April 30, 1870), "Bush Ballads and Galloping
Rhymes" (June 25, 1870, the day after Gordon's suicide), "The
Courtly Poets" (July 9, 1870) and "Rossetti's Poetry" (July 23, 1870).
But, by his own admission, these successes were won with difficulty,
for it was hard to convince newspaper editors to use "space and
capital for articles that the large body of the public would never take
the trouble to glance at."[1]

I Some Literary Comments

After his return to Sydney in 1870 Kendall became a regular con-
tributor to the *Freeman's Journal* and "The Harp of Erin" series by
him included feature articles on Irish writers, Thomas Davis,
Clarence Mangan, Thomas D'Arcy McGee, J. J. Callanan, Samuel
Ferguson and others. This series ran from September 2 to November
11, 1871. A new series "Notes Upon Men and Books" began in the
same journal on December 2, 1871.

Number three in the "Notes Upon Men and Books" series was a rather audacious attack on the poetry of Walt Whitman. Kendall knew too little about Whitman's poetry to offer a worthwhile analysis, but he objected strongly to Whitman's experiments, assessing the American's poetry as "a sort of wild recitative controlled by no known technical laws; set down without regard to metre, rhythm, or anything else that we have been accustomed to associate with our notions of verse." He quoted Whitman's lines:

> Three scythes at harvest whizzing in a row, from three
>   lusty angels with shirts bagged out at their waists.
>
> The snag-toothed ostler with red hair redeeming past
>   sins and sins to come,
>
> Selling all he possesses, travelling on foot to fee
>   lawyers for his brother, and sit by him while he is
>   tried for forgery,

and maintained that he could not "see any good reason why the very excellent prose . . . should be chopped into pieces to give it the aspect of indifferent verse." He was scandalized by Whitman's lines:

> For the one I loved most lay sleeping by me under the
>   same cover in the cool night;
> In the stillness — in the autumn moonbeams, his face
>   was inclined towards me,
> And his arm lay lightly around my breast, and that
>   night I was happy.

His indignation erupted in the horrified but amusing comment about "one unsavoury Yankee democrat hugging and spooning with another."[2] Number eight in this series contributed further valuable details of the literary activities of Daniel Deniehy, "Peter Possum" (Richard Rowe), "the Peripatetic Philosopher" (Marcus Clarke) and offered a succinct and accurate observation of Gordon's poetry — "he was clearly not a poet in the sense Harpur was. The latter had a large share of that rare gift, the creative faculty, whereas Gordon had not a spark of it."[3]

II *Kendall's View of the Colonial Literary Scene*

Kendall's frustration at his failure to make a living through his literary talent is illustrated in the repeated complaint in his poetry of the "life austere" that confronted the man of letters in the colony. This theme of colonial apathy toward the local writer also occupied several of his prose writings, especially during the bitter experiences of 1872 and in the resentful years that followed his recovery. His first extended commentary came in "Men of Letters in New South Wales" published in *Punch Staff Papers,* 1872:

While every possible effort has been made by the colony for the attainment of physical prosperity and wealth almost next to nothing has been done with regard to its intellectual advance; or, in other words, towards the creation and fostering of a native literature. . . . While we have had, and have still, men amongst us with sufficient native power to become the fathers of a striking antipodean literature, there has been little, if anything, achieved towards its creation. . . . I will now proceed to sketch the austere situation occupied till this day by the colonial literates. With one or two exceptions, the whole of them are poor; and most of them have no means of livelihood other than the pen. . . . What then is the history of these people — these men acknowledged to be 'clever', and assuredly in straitened circumstances? Simply this. Many — indeed the most of them, enter the field while mere youths, full of enthusiasm, elated with the consciousness that in the unique life and scenery around them they can find ample material for the exercise of their respective gifts; but the end invariably is disappointment and sorrow. They very soon come to realise that Australia is a new country; that society here is still in an unsettled chaotic state; that the large bulk of the population have yet to get their money before they can enjoy leisure; that the wealthy classes — the geebung aristocracy, as they are called — are formed for the most part of illiterate people, who have risen from the ranks; and, in short, that there is not the ghost of a chance for a writer attempting to get his living by offering to the public work not lying within the domains of journalism. So it comes to pass that those who happen to be lucky enough, and who possess the necessary aptitude, join the Press, and in due time forget their early aspirations and become plodding, satisfied newspaper hacks. The men who are not so fortunate — God help them![4]

Such an attitude — that the world owed him and his literary fellows a living — was neither sensible nor manly. If Kendall had bothered to recall the life histories of many of the great traditional literary figures he would have found many who had faced, and overcome, far greater problems. However unattractive his tone of complaint is, his analysis of the colonial situation has considerable historical and literary interest. In attaching the blame for contemporary neglect of himself and his fellow writers he was surprisingly generous to the working and middle classes who "have to make their money before they can rest and read" and the "illiterate wealthy" who know no better, for "grapes are never found growing on thistles." Nor did he attribute the blame to the Press which "consists entirely of newspapers dependent upon men who discover more music in the clink of a coin than in the grandest symphony Beethoven ever composed, and who rarely look inside a book." His acrimony was directed at a class whom he came more and more to envy (and despise) for their smug, protective cloak of birth, position and learning. He blamed

that influential class in our midst who are lettered as well as leisured; and from whom accredited colonial writers naturally expect countenance. A just recognition on the part of these men — these scholars, university professors, judges, barristers etc. — *a just recognition and nothing more* — would help the cause of Australian polite letters to a degree that they themselves have no conception of. To put the matter in a clearer light, the countenance of scholars moving amongst the wealthier circles of the community would so influence the ignorant, and therefore credulous, rich that they would come to buy, for the sake of show, that which they might never read. But the people thus having it in their power to develop our intellectual resources — the great grammarians who walk to and fro in society with the dignified air of the elder gods — seem wilfully to have come to the determination to ignore them altogether. For example, I have heard more than one scholar question the *necessity* for Australian *belles-lettres*. Why, they have asked, should we foster a new and immature growth when we have the magnificent literary possessions of the old country at hand? By this they infer an intention on our part to create a literature utterly independent of what is justly a source of pride to Englishmen; but we have no such purpose in our heads. What colonial men of letters are anxious to do ought to be obvious enough. They look upon the grand results of British genius with as much exalted joy as their fathers did; but, at the same time, they naturally desire to take advantage of the novel elements by which they are surrounded, and to gather from these (speaking figuratively) fresh sap for the ancient stock.

Some of Kendall's dislike of this "superior" class of academics and professional men sprang from his envy of them, from his awareness that he was an "outsider," and neither by birth nor learning could he break into their circle of privilege. His charges against them, however, were largely true. It was their particular brand of intellectual snobbery that frustrated the efforts of local writers to contribute toward the creation of a new national literature and it led to the infuriated backlash of the *Bulletin* and the nationalists not many years later.

Kendall returned to the theme again in "Old Manuscripts" in the *Freeman's Journal*, November 17, 1877. He did not accept it as automatic that literary genius brings literary success, yet success in the sense of respect and recognition of his work is the main goal that the writer strives for. Failure to achieve that goal desolates the sensitive writer. He illustrates his text by an initial reference to Clarence Mangan, "a singer whose gifts entitled him to the very highest place amongst Irish poets from Amergin downwards . . . a supreme bard who dies with his name indeed written in water." The trend of his thoughts is clearly, however, toward his own case for he correlates Mangan's history with

that of many young men who have entered the domains of literature with real acquirements — real ability; but without the bodily stamina, and assistance from worldly surroundings, to carry them to the goal of their desire. Born under an unlucky star; deprived by the necessity for labour of that large leisure which is indispensable to Art; frozen with apathy, where they expected encouragement; they have either forsaken the field of their first endeavours, or perished in a barren struggle to overcome opposing influences.[5]

From the injured, plaintive tone of these articles it appears that Kendall's main ambition was to be one of a leisured literary class who could be absolved from the humdrum cares and anxieties of life while his talent quietly and satisfyingly matured. It was a totally unrealistic attitude for the time; and it is almost as unrealistic even today. Usually in these critical articles he cited the cases of Daniel Deniehy and Charles Harpur as the classic examples of neglect. Referring to his own situation he claims to have "left the fields of literature forever." He is now nothing but a "literary hack" (the pseudonym he used for many of his articles), yet there was a time when he was "as full of the poetical dream as was Shelley." He was driven from that dream by disappointments in the field of letters and by the need to earn his bread by bitter labor.

It was seldom wise in that age (or in any other for that matter) for a writer to vent his spleen publicly against the newspaper editors who sat in judgment on the contributions submitted for publication. In 1878 Kendall apparently felt himself beyond the reach of retaliation for there is, in "The August Windeyer" (the *Freeman's Journal*, Febrary 9, 1878), a scornful commentary on the *Sydney Morning Herald*, "Grannie" of Hunter Street. The memory of humiliations suffered in earlier years sharpens the satirical edge of his pen.

My memory travels back into the dusk domains of dear dead years when I was a bright-eyed youth, with more enthusiasm than knowledge of the world in general, and of "Grannie" in particular. Then I used to inflict "literature" on her — "literature" for which she has forgotten to pay . . . With my mind's eye I seem to see her well-known office and her old bulbous editor. A fine aroma of the tabernacle pervades the chamber, dashed with a horsey fragrance from the tights of a sporting reporter. I am happy because — according to the dream — my little contribution has been graciously accepted. It is — let it be noted — a gratuitous "sling in." While I stand measuring myself mentally with Dickens and Thackeray, and gazing with obvious awe on the greater light, the oleaginous West, a stranger enters the sanctuary. . . . I know this man well, because his astonishing attainments, and equally marvellous native abilities, are themes of everyday conversation with his countrymen. In my vision I clearly recognize the matchless orator — brilliant man of letters — perfect artist, and encyclopaedical scholar, who goes by the name, *Daniel Henry Deniehy*. He offers my globular West a manuscript, and falteringly asks for twenty shillings — the price he puts on the document. I do not know its contents — it is probably a paper on medieval art. The face of the bold editor goes to show that it is neither the report of a "tea fight" nor a salacious description of a bagnio [brothel]. Consequently, it is declined with not too many thanks; and the issue of its writer's application for coin is a rough "good morning sir". . . . poor beggar, he was only a scholar and a man of genius![6]

III *Satirical Articles*

Kendall emerged from the tormented years of 1872 - 73 with a jaundiced view of the whole colonial scene. There was nothing left of the wide-eyed idealist of the early 1860s. He selected for particular asperity of comment those areas of public life where he felt cant and humbug were most freely flourishing — politics and religion. It was in the *Freeman's Journal* that his vitriolic verses such as "The Gagging Bill" were published and in it also, under a variety of pseudonyms, he continued to attack, in the most unabashed fashion, prominent people of the day. Typical of his satirical articles were "An Election in Shamshire" (December 8, 1877); "Political Biographies. By A Literary Hack. No. 1 The Limber Lucas" (February 2, 1878); "Political Biographies. By A Literary Hack. No. 2 The August Windeyer"; "The Triple Headed Coalition. A Drama in One Act" (February 23, 1878); and "Jones — A Biography — By The Mopoke" (October, 19, 1880).

"Jones — A Biography — By The Mopoke" is a thinly disguised criticism of R. B. Smith, the member for Camden Haven, who annoyed Kendall by seldom bothering to call, even at election time, upon his constituents. Kendall, and others, in a practical joke, persuaded a local shingle-splitter, Tom Amos, to stand against Smith in the elections, a move that soon brought Smith to defend his seat. Kendall says in the article that he has lost a highly flattering biography of Jones which was published in a recent newspaper and so sets out to write a new and more factual account of member Jones's life and character. As a student Jones was such a conspicuous failure that his mentor (Kendall's old friend J. Sheridan Moore) advised him:

You have no brains, my boy — we'll take that for granted; but then, you have coin; and if you want to be a big man your path is as plain as the purple on my nose. Your "dart" is Parliament; and in order to work into that illustrious shop, you must knock round every corner — mount every possible stump, and pitch up your voice in every backdoor taproom, and at every hole-and-corner meeting. It is probable that you will have nothing to say; but, by all means, *say it*. Then as good society is necessary in the matter, tip the big wigs, and — *there you are*. When the proper time shall have arrived, "run" for some backwoods constituency; crack round on the Cheater racket, and by all means let the "cannikan clink."[7]

The similarity of "Jones — A Biography" to the censored poem "The Song of Ninian Melville" is obvious. Kendall's animus against politicians and other public figures was intense and his attacks on them were stingingly personal. Either he bore a grudge against people like Sir Henry Parkes, R. B. Smith and Ninian Melville because of envy of their high and apparently lucrative offices or because he felt that his own achievements had had insufficient public recognition and deflating these people gave him some perverse kind of satisfaction. If these are extreme views — a close study of Kendall's life suggests no other — then the only explanation of his persistent attacks in his later years against these men must be that he failed to suffer fools gladly, especially those who, in his opinion, were corrupt fools in high places.

IV *Descriptive Prose*

Kendall's talent for natural description is less obvious in his prose than in his poetry but the occasional descriptive articles are a pleasant relief from the welter of complaints and satires that poured from his pen. Before he left Gosford in 1875 he wrote a long description of the Brisbane Water country for two issues of the *Town and Country Journal*, February 27, and March 6, 1875.

... the central picture is Narrara Creek, a stately river-like stream rising in the ranges of "Mangrove" and falling by two mouths into Brisbane Water, opposite Gosford. Winding like some splendid serpent of the pre-Adamite days, amongst such hills as I have been describing, it seems the lone live thing of the place — the one vocal feature of the wilderness ... About six miles to the west of Narrara lies the darkly magnificent valley of Mooni Mooni. Shut in by immense beetling hills from half the morning; hiding an April in the hottest days of December; and cooling the eye with a blessing of brooks when the tops of the ridge are dead for want of rain, this beautiful Goshen is still left to those primitive types, the sawyer and shingle-splitter — and to a few of these only. Nature jealously defends her stronghold here with cliff and chasm and torrent and a phalanx of forest on whose wet green recesses the sun never shines. Here, and at the sources of the Wy-Wy and Narrara, are those deep heavy-wood ravines that you find in the heart of Kembla — awful abysses showing yet the track of the earthquake, and the fierce epitaph written by fire on ruined precipices. ... But where the grand is, there is also the beautiful. The moss — that green, tender thing which softens so the asperity of the grave-stone — the great glittering ferns which love to live out of sight — those graceful vegetable parasites that gather life and strength from barren rocks — that lovely Semela of the wilderness, the bangalow, too delicate for the embrace of the sun, the myrtle, the sassafras, and all the affluent vegetation that thrives best in the darkness, are there. There also are the strong notes of the waterfall, the joyous cry of the prosperous torrents, the echoes of innumerable clefts, and the delicious tones of the bell-bird which

> 'Smite
> Crisp air with clarions of delight'

There the wind rarely wanders; and there the roar of the tempest on the ranges sounds like the melancholy wail that one seems to hear in the august Arthurian epos.

Kendall adapts his descriptive prose style admirably to the particular image he wishes to convey. Where the landscape is grim, chaotic and confused, as it is in the rugged, precipitous Brisbane Water reaches, his prose becomes cramped, compacted, almost tortured. "Immense fragments of rock, cunningly carved by that sublime sculptor, Water — gigantic boulders tossed here and there in most fantastical confusion — night-like gaps giving up the song of unseen torrents — caves of stalactite and stalagmite vaulted and groined like a cathedral — domes like the relics of a mighty Druidical temple — these form the dominant features of those valleys."[8] His description in the same journal, May 5, 1881, of the stately Manning River district where he went to live after his appointment as Inspector of Forests is, on the other hand, elegant, graceful prose.

My new home is a place of gracious greeness — a land of soft cool lawns fall-ing away into crescents of radiant river. I write this in sight of a stream whose beauty makes the heart ache. South and west of me lies a spacious tract — a great yellow sea of growing maize dotted here and there with snug, comfortable-looking dwelling houses. North and east are vast clear grassy plains running away into a background of remote forest. In the dis-tant west, far beyond the flash and ring of river stands a magnificent range of mountains: and the stately peaks of these complete a picture of marvellous beauty.[9]

V *Kendall's Letters to Charles Harpur*

Considerable information on the earlier colonial poet, Charles Harpur, is contained in Kendall's numerous references to him in the twenty years between the beginning of their correspondence in 1862 and Kendall's own death in 1882. The "old manuscripts" that Ken-dall referred to in the title of the *Freeman's Journal* article in 1877 were those of Harpur. In an earlier article, "About Some Men of Letters in Australia" (the *Australian Journal*, October, 1869), he had given the only physical description that there is of Harpur. The Ken-dall penchant for the dramatic is evident but the portrait is valuable nevertheless:

I met Harpur for the first time about six months before his death. He was then suffering from the earlier effects of the disease which terminated so fatally; and he appeared to be the almost empty shell of his former self. He had the frame, and must have had in younger days, the strength of a giant. The man was a noble ruin — one that had been scorched and wasted as it were, by fire. His face looked as if it had been through the hottest fur-naces of sorrow; indeed it reminded me of Coleridge's description of a countenance whose strange, almost terrible, weariness told of agonies that had been, and were, and were still to continue to be.

He contrasts, in "Old Manuscripts," the general neglect of Harpur with the impact that poet made on some of his more thoughtful and intellectual contemporaries; but the discussion of several Harpur poems, including one of Kendall's favorites, "Gramachree," is brief and superficial. The piece concludes, not untypically, with this fulsome comment:

Poor Harpur! . . . His "Native land" has forgotten him . . . his grave at Nerrigundah is an unnoticed one. But he sleeps in the august forest, by the side of the beautiful stream that he loved so well . . . Over this last home of his, the wild oak — that elphin [sic] harp of the solitudes — iterates its mysterious music year after year. . . . But the elders of his generation have forgotten him; and their sons have never heard of him. Among mighty and monumental men there is no place for him: his seat in the temple is close to the doorways. Under favouring auspices he might have completed the statue — as it was, he left us *only the foot of Hercules.*

Kendall seemed, in these public statements, in contrast to the sound critical judgments which he often made in private letters, more interested in grandiloquent, sentimentalizing flourishes than in penetrative, worthwhile commentary.

Henry Kendall's letters have been useful in authenticating his own biographical data and in accurately dating and interpreting many of his poems. On the whole, however, his correspondence is disappointing. Clarke's evaluation of it in his unpublished thesis, "A Critical Edition of the Letters of Henry Kendall," is that:

The contribution the letters make to the history of public events, to the general history of Australian culture in the nineteenth century, and, in particular, to the history of literary taste in Australia, is very meagre. . . . These letters are almost totally devoid of descriptions or even pointed references to public events and public figures. There is no account of politics despite the great vitality and formative importance of it during Kendall's life-time; no account of, or comment on the great explorations; almost nothing about the theatre which in Kendall's day was enjoying a fierce popularity; very little about the public service of which Kendall was, for a time, a member. There is no mention of the "Yellow Scare" of the Seventies; of the Seamen's Strike of '78, against coloured labour; of the opening of the railways; of the development of public education.[10]

There were good reasons for the absence of such themes from Kendall's letters. The personal problems of his young manhood absorbed much of his time and energy in those years; the "Shadow of 1872" led him to withdraw from public contact in the middle period of his life; and in his final years his remoteness in country areas kept him from close participation in the events of the day.

Kendall's letters to Charles Harpur are a welcome exception to Clarke's general observation. The most interesting area of his correspondence, in both a literary and historical sense, is the exchange of letters between him and Harpur over a period of almost six years, from January, 1862, until Harpur's death, June 10, 1868. The correspondence began with Kendall's letter of January 8, 1862, although some contact appears to have been established earlier, probably through Kendall's expression of his interest in Harpur's poetry to Joseph Harpur, the poet's brother, who represented Patrick's Plains in the New South Wales Legislative Assembly. This first letter reveals Kendall's youthful admiration for Harpur, his elevation of him to the position of national poet and hints of Harpur's unavailing fight for recognition:

I recieved [sic] the two poems that you were kind enough to forward to me, and deemed it my duty to thank you directly. So you must excuse the liberty I am taking in writing to you, and the peculiar hand adopted here. Your brother, Mr. Joseph Harpur, will tell you that I am obliged to indite my letters in this fashion, my right arm being lame. About two months ago Mr. Piddington gave me a volume of yours. Since then I have passed many a delightful evening poring over it. Amongst your numerous sincere admirers there are none more sincere than myself; and I rejoice that I have mind enough to appreciate you.

You have a noble soul which never appears to be baffled, though it has so long worked against opposition and unkindness. I grow sick when listening to people talking about "the unfortunate Keats", and the "sorrows of Chatterton" — remembering your brave life. . . . Your influence is beginning to be felt and it is to be regretted that you have been so silent lately. I speak for the rising generation of Australians who are far more intellectual than their predecessors, and who *must* turn to you, as I have already done, with the love and reverence which is due to their national poet. . . .

It was more than eight months before Kendall received a reply to his first letter. Harpur pleaded the pressure of affairs. Kendall had spent the intervening period seeking out Harpur's poems in the *Empire* files to add to those which he had met in the volume *The Bushrangers: A Play in Five Acts, and Other Poems*, published in 1853. In this second letter, September 25, 1862, he began his assessment of particular Harpur poems, and his comments have, in this century, provided valuable clues to the dating and location of early Harpur writing. The letter begins with his apt comment about the gains he would expect from correspondence with Harpur:

. . . we cannot leave a cedar grove without carrying away some of the fragrance, and the words of Genius may be fitly associated with the perfume — scattering leaves of those trees. I feel already deeply indebted to you for the great good and large comfort I have derived from your writings. There is no living author to whom I could turn and say as much. This may be a necessary result of my Australian birth and education. But, strangely fascinated by almost everything you have published, I have always looked upon you as the man who alone could express what I had so often dimly thought. While looking round upon external nature, *some* of us see and feel *that* which we afterwards lose sight of and forget, until we find it, photographed as it were, in the luminous "limning" of the true poet.

The same letter contains Kendall's assertion (mentioned in chapter 3) that the most rare endowment of the poet is the gift of "exact expression," since with it he can reveal the whole truth that is within him in "unclouded simplicity." It contains also his expression of affinity (referred to also in chapter 3) with Harpur's protagonist, Egremont, in "The Creek of the Four Graves." He continues with commentary on other Harpur poems:

The "Tower of the Dream" is another of my favourites. One of the similes in that poem is the finest I have met with *anywhere*; and the song of the Spirit is so wildly — so strangely beautiful that one *might* imagine it to be conceived, as 'Kubla Khan' was, in a Dream. I don't care much for "Yes" — one of Mr. Stenhouse's pets — but "Mary", "In Yon Green Wood", and "Cora", are indeed lovely. This, from "Cora", haunts me whenever I turn to the sunset:

> "Bright garments of a Spirit bright,
> That even in the shroud
> Were like the sunset's golden light
> Within a lifeless cloud!"

"Finish of Style" has all the "bloom of unhandled grapes" about it, and the second of your "Poems of Melancholy" sounds the very depths of feeling. I do not care much for what has been printed of "Genius Lost", although there are so many fine passages in it. Perhaps it proceeds from my having no great sympathy for Chatterton. You must forgive me for being so candid. The extracts from "King Saul" have truly a rich Oriental flush around them, and are as odorous as the cedars of Lebanon.

A year and a half after Kendall's first letter he subtly changed the relationship between them by offering to help with Harpur's plans for "A Proposed Volume of Poems." He said, July 4, 1863, "I could be of some service to you in Sydney having knowledge of many wealthy men who profess to admire you exceedingly." Later, October 26, 1863, he received from Harpur a critical piece, "Blank Verse," which he declared he would get published in the *Herald* and in the next letter, November 3, 1863, he virtually became Harpur's

Sydney agent, indicating that "anything you may wish to see in print I will gladly insert in the *Herald* for you."

He continued his discussion, August 16, 1863, of Harpur's poetry by commenting on a group of sonnets that Harpur had sent him:

"Poetry" is familiar, through the published volume; "The First Great Australian Poet" is *rocky*. "True and False Glory", although good, was written at a time, I think, when your "singing robes" were not on. "Charity" brims over with tenderness. These are lovely lines: —

"On thy maternal bosom many a time
I lay my head and dream that yet thy reign
In its faith-widen'd influence every clime
Shall sweeten; and, as o'er some torrid plain
Fresh air breathe vigor, quicken Man to attain
Capacity for Love's millenial prime."

"The Tear" is the most musical of the seven. It is full of *tearful* Pathos. I like it even better than "Love's Star" notwithstanding the investiture of more than one beautiful thought in the latter. It, Love's Star, was evidently born of this:

"The Star of Evening is a gracious feature,
Instinct as 'twere with all the Love that eyes
Have looked through at the skies."

In the seventh sonnet, and in your last letter to me, you express keen discontent with regard to your present lot. I can well understand how a Poet must suffer, the hair of whose head is turning grey in the chilling blasts of Neglect. But this Neglect is only ephemeral — and the author of the "Tower of the Dream" is no butterfly. He ought to be all-sufficient for the troubled Present, who has such a goodly heritage in the clear future. If any one asked me to point out Harpur's most characteristic poem, I should turn to the "Tower of the Dream". Yet I speak, very likely, out of a limited knowledge of your writings. I don't forget the "Creek of the Four Graves" when my belief is stated that the "Tower of the Dream" is the greatest of Australian poems and one of the finest of its kind in the English language. The Dream-Song is instinct with Dream-Music. "Freedom in Faith" has the roll of an unknown sea in it. "Records of Romantic Passion" should be read in a mountain glen, at night, with a glimpse of "moonsilvered sea" far, far away. These are your greatest sonnets. I hate praising a man to his face. . . . But in talking to a Poet who is wholly without the sympathy which he *must* look for, I do not unrighteously bridle my tongue.

Three days later, August 19, 1863, he wrote again, having received four more sonnets from Harpur, with his impressions of the new verses:

The one addressed to that fine fellow, Andrew Marvell, is my favourite. "A Worldling" is very effective. "My Faith in Poetry" could only have been written by one fully conscious of his *Life* in Poetry. And of the rare felicity in that Life above a Life. "The Poverty of Genius" is perhaps the wisest of the lot. With regard to the *rhyme* and *construction* of your Sonnets I will here say a few words: —

The rhyme arrangement I like exceedingly. Through its agency each line dies off like a seawave. I have often wondered about the origin of this form so distinct from the Italian.

You construct many of your sonnets with an utter disregard for superficial harmony. They are about as uneven as a rain-rutted mountain crag. Yet there is for me, a wild beauty in this ruggedness. I don't remember having met with anywhere, a Sonnet which has impressed me more than yours headed "Freedom in Faith". What a grand *undertone* rolls through it! Wordsworth has written nothing finer.

In the same letter to Harpur he discussed Tennyson (see chapter 3 above) and some time later referred to Cowper in the course of a general discussion on poetry:

I have been reading Cowper lately, and I like him the better for renewed acquaintance. He is a Master of Pathos — indeed where he is immediate like the author of Elaine he sweetens the mind with sorrow. I do not care for his narrative passages, nor have I much regard for his descriptions of scenery. He can very prettily describe, for instance, a nook or a bend in the river, but he cannot set it 'lightening on' as someone says, from source to mouth in a single line as Thomson or Tennyson could. In fact in this last respect he is elaborate but not adequate. He stands as it were shivering on the brink of Beauty, yet only on the brink. But in the Poetry of Retrospection where the personal element is prominent he is almost unapproachable. And this kind of verse is for ever happy. . . . Poetry has very often been the means of a man's salvation. I believe it has prevented me from falling many a time. . . . I recognize in Poetry a revelation of Divinity beyond all revelations, a religion past religion. Mind you I do not include in this name Verse alone but all Harmony, whether it be through Music, Verse or Prose. When I face the face of things, through the eyes of this Agent, I am, as it were, an *Aboriginal* man. I look about me, as one might have looked on the first morning of creation, with a surpassing wonder. The Visible seems everlastingly new — everlastingly suggestive. There is a gloss for me on things — a gloss which once seen, never leaves a man without the companionship and exceeding great comfort of Beauty.[11]

Kendall grew in time to be extremely critical of the colonial writers who combined little talent with inflated egos, yet his attitude was more generous at this time than Harpur's. Such writers included Halloran, Michael, Stenhouse and others from the literary and university coterie of Sydney. He disliked them but wisely saw that in the contemporary colonial literary scene they had a role to play, as he commented in his letter, October 26, 1863: "As cordially as yourself do I set my face against the pretenders who are only notorious for their pretensions. But these men are somehow necessary in their way: they do all the needful brooming in dirty corners. Literature could not thrive without them."

During 1864 and early 1865 the correspondence with Harpur languished. It was April, 1865, before it recommenced. Harpur was constantly polishing and varying his verses. An example of this habit is seen in one letter, May 10, 1865, where he encloses a reprint of "an old poem . . . with some retouches and additions." Harpur reassured Kendall about this tendency to pick at his verses — "I try all the alterations I make *as by fire.*" Kendall had voiced his doubts about Harpur's tendency in the letter of April 29, 1865:

There is at all times a charm about the rough rock that we cannot discover in the polished mason-work. . . . You must forgive me for my overfear lest the 'freshness of the morning prime' should be sullied in the least where it is so pure and so abundant. Let 'The Tower of the Dream' stand for us, as we know it. Never doubt its immortality; but for the sake of hereafter delights, keep a jealous watch over its present integrity. I believe it is the highest result of your genius. It is even a Wonder Dream more wondrous than "Kubla Khan".

Kendall's admiration for "The Tower of the Dream," a long poem in blank verse interspersed with songs, caused Harpur to have it printed separately as a pamphlet. The poem has not received the same acclaim from others critics, Donovan Clarke decrying it, Judith Wright never quite coming to grips with her own attitudes to it but believing that it shows Harpur to have been "a thinking, rather than a lyrical, poet."[12] Kendall was obsessed with "The Tower." He made a series of comments, "marginalia," mentioning them to Harpur, December 2, 1865: "The Tower is very much admired. In my next I will send you a printed copy with my particular 'marginalia' against noted passages. I do not know whether I am competent to judge upon the work but perhaps I am one of the best you can get out here." The "marginalia" he refers to is preserved in the Mitchell Library in a manuscript book of Kendalliana and consists of some curious but interesting comments on what Kendall saw as the notable passages in the poem.

Harpur's "Gramachree" was one of his particular favorites among the individual poems: "Have you not heard, in your forest walks, a wild broken wind, which, after a day of shattered life had fallen down to its softer evening passages? Have you not heard then a recurring sound forever like the sound of a fitful Aeolian Harp? You *have* and therefore 'Gramachree', full of the 'red' sunset and perplexed with a perplexing sorrow was written. Its beauty makes the heart ache."[13] Familiarity brought a measure of licence. He grew irritated with Harpur's idiosyncratic spelling, August 26, 1865, reading him a small homily on the subject:

I am at issue with you in the matter of your late mannerisms in orthography. Why not spell "hony" honey? Certain peculiarities of this kind somewhat mar the effect of your finer poems. Very likely you have the best of reasons for those new methods of writing words but I cannot well see why the Poet should be a mere lexicographer. He is a maker and adapter of languages but hardly an arranger of letters. After all the best objection to your novelties is the objection of the everyday reader. To him you would convey a *consecutive* pleasure through your poem and yet you force him to break over a mere word in the middle of a noble passage of dreams. Why should the "Tower of the Dream" in the least degree suggest a dispute over orthography? I think familiar words ought to be spelled in a familiar way.

To Harpur, ill later in the same year, he offered the comfort, "Never fear for your ultimate recognition by your fellows. It will come as surely as tomorrow's sun." November 28, 1865, saw the publication of "The Tower." Kendall could not resist some final comments: " 'The Tower' is at last published but not in the 'Empire'. Somehow the people of that paper did not like the 'Tower', it was too massive for them. They backed out of the printing of it by urging that their precious *daub* was a 'commercial and not a literary journal'. . . . Your poem 'The Tower of the Dream' shines like a bit of Shelley at his best, in print. It is beyond all doubt your most characteristic work." By 1867 Harpur had become bitterly frustrated by his neglect at the hands of the critics. He had also lost his son in the autumn of that year in a shooting accident and had been retrenched from his government position as gold commissioner. In one of the last letters that Kendall wrote to him he attempted to console the forlorn poet, October 8, 1867: "You overrate newspaper people by expecting them to see the great beauty and the genuine power of your writings. The public to which your poems will appeal is not in existence yet, but its advent is inevitable. . . . If a striking originality wedded to the music of waters and the strength of thunder is only necessary to constitute the first great Australian Poet, certainly the author of 'The Tower' and 'The Witch of Hebron' may lay claim to the crown."

These letters to Harpur enshrine opinions which though not completely vindicated by the intervening years, have done much to keep Harpur's reputation alive. To what extent they are the fulsome praise of the young poetic disciple toward the master or the astute, perceptive criticism of a highly sensitive poetic intelligence only the final assessment of Harpur will reveal.

Although Kendall's prose writings are of no great literary merit in themselves they derive considerable historical and literary interest from his position as the leading colonial poet of the time. The numerous articles in which he commented at length on the role and position of the colonial writers are a valuable addition to the sparse record of the literary scene in the decades 1850 to 1880. His analyses of the emerging English, Irish and American poets are unlikely to be preserved in future anthologies of criticism but they reveal a most perceptive literary intelligence, one keen to encounter both old and new literary experiences, and courageous, or brash, enough to make judgments of those experiences, judgments which have proved to be original and reasonably valid. His later newspaper articles he appeared to take lightly, referring privately to them somewhat contemptuously as "squibs" and "trifles." They were eagerly sought by editors and he was paid much more for them than for his poetry — a fact which ironically substantiated his view that, to make a living, a literary man had to become a "literary hack." There is little interest for modern readers in his vendetta against some of the personalities of the time but his satirical prose does highlight (as did his verses) the waspish, aggressive attitudes of his later years.

CHAPTER 6

Kendall in Perspective

H ENRY KENDALL was the last of the Australian colonial poets. His death in 1882 marks the watershed between the end of the colonial era in literature and the upsurge of nationalism. The colonial period produced only three significant poets, Charles Harpur, Adam Lindsay Gordon and Kendall, all of whom, except for one slim volume by Harpur in 1845, wrote after midcentury. Before 1850 there was little worthwhile local poetry, and virtually none that took its tone from, and reflected the attitudes of, the new Australian environment. Michael Massey Robinson's annual odes from 1810 in celebration of the birthdays of George III and Queen Charlotte indicated the colony's loyalty to England but showed only a passing awareness of the local scene. Robinson drew brief attention to the aborigines as "yon sable race" and to the distant Blue Mountains as "the craggy cliffs that guard the ling'-ring Waste." William Charles Wentworth, the first Australian-born poet, in his prize poem "Australasia," written while he was at Cambridge in 1823, saw his native land as "a new Britannia in another world." Charles Tompson, born in the colony, was the first poet to have a volume of poems published here, but his *Wild Notes, from the Lyre of a Native Minstrel*, 1826, is more the verse of a transplanted Englishman than a "native minstrel."

From the beginning local writers had difficulty making an impact on the colonial scene. The main problem was colonial disinterest in cultural matters. The materialism of the time is summed up in Kenneth Slessor's words:

It was an age when a man who had enough sheep or cattle or land could become as rich as Tommy Mort, get a house like Burdekin's, drive a plum-coloured brougham like Jeremiah Rundle's without even having to learn how to sign his name except with a mark. The circle of politicians, lawyers, journalists, medical men, professional men and rich collectors of the arts who brought books of poetry or talked about English literature and the art of writing was a mere fraction of the population. To the others the art of writing must have seemed as useless and occult as the art of playing an Assyrian sackbut.[1]

Colonial apathy was toward literature in general but toward local writers and local literature in particular — as Kendall repeatedly observed. Colonial writers were also subjected to confusing extremes of critical treatment. Some critics of the day measured colonial writing solely against the established excellence of the finest traditional literature. Although this was not, in theory, an unfair yardstick it was certainly a rigorous one and it led inevitably to the depreciation of colonial literature. These critics also seemed to feel that the colonial writer was inferior simply because he *was* colonial. This particular brand of intellectual snobbery led to local writers being either derided or ignored. The opposite tendency, of other critics, to overvalue local talent, was equally harmful. Apparently feeling that any colonial literary sound was preferable to silence they judged too generously. This was especially true with the occasional local writer of quality who, clearly superior to his colonial contemporaries, came to be equated with the accepted masters of English literature.

Harpur and Gordon are particular examples of the extremes of this erratic critical treatment. Harpur, writing in an early colonial environment when society was still in an unsettled state and the exigencies of life allowed little scope for any form of cultural activity, had very little sympathetic critical opinion to advise and encourage him. His origins and circumstances were against him. He was the son of a convict in a land still largely a convict colony. The notion that worthwhile poetry could come from such a man in such an environment was regarded as absurd. Yet Kendall's judgment that "if Harpur had been born in an old and settled society and had been helped by favourable circumstances, he would have produced some everlasting work" is probably a true assessment of a striking literary talent which went largely unrecognized because of the accidents of time and place. Harpur passed from enthusiastic endeavour to frustration to disillusion to bitter gloom. In 1867, a year before his death, he sardonically penned his own epitaph:

Here lies Charles Harpur, who at fifty years of age [he was actually fifty-four] came to the conclusion, that he was living in a sham age, under a sham

Government, and amongst sham friends, and that any World whatever must therefore be a better world than theirs. And having come to this conclusion, he did his dying and now lies here with one of his sons, in the hope of their meeting in some place better fitted to make them happy, and to keep them so, than this from which they have departed. And even if all that now remains of them is what remains below — it is still well: inasmuch as, in that case, they are safe from all malignity, whether proceeding from God or Devil, that would further afflict them.[2]

Adam Lindsay Gordon criticism provides a contrasting picture, perhaps the best example of unbridled local partiality. Most of Gordon's poetry, leaving aside the occasional competent piece of traditional balladry and the rare glimpse of his affinity with his new Australian environment, is so meager either in poetic quality or thematic substance that it remains, today, deservedly unread. Yet it was used in the decade or so after his death to claim for him a literary greatness to which he had no right. It was said that "in the whole range of English literature there have been few poets possessed of a finer lyrical faculty than Adam Lindsay Gordon. . . . 'Ashtaroth' is worthy to rank with any of Tennyson's songs"[3] and Alexander Sutherland has written that "Gordon's poems are among the best in the English language that the last twenty years can boast of . . . there is no one who is Gordon's superior in true poetic fire. We may, if we choose, rank Rossetti and Swinburne and Matthew Arnold, and the Morrises as high or higher but it will not be by virtue of that homethrusting power of genuine poetry . . . for sheer poetry there is none to compare with Gordon."[4]

So monumental were these critical blunders, born from an anxious desire to crown a "Monarch of Australian Song," that reaction was swift and sustained. By 1900 Gordon was adjudged "rather a versifier . . . than a true poet"; and in 1912 A. G. Stephens was classifying him as merely "a horse-poet." Contemporary opinion would agree with Judith Wright's assessment of him as "no more than mediocre."[5] The deflation of Gordon, however, has never been completely achieved. The nationalists were especially keen to salvage the popular notion of him as Australia's first national poet. There was an instant charisma in the romantic circumstances of his life — the apparent rejection of his aristocratic background in favour of the egalitarian Australian life, his flamboyant exploits in the saddle in a land where horses and horsemanship were much appreciated, and finally, the pathos of his death. There was a sense of gratitude too among the nationalists for Gordon's acclaim, in a poem such as "The

Sick Stockrider," of a way of life which they recognized and accepted as their own. In the words of Barcroft Boake in 1889: "There is not a bushman or a drover who does not know a verse or two of 'How We Beat the Favourite' or 'The Sick Stockrider'. . . . Gordon is the favourite — I may say the only — poet of the backblocker."[6] In the long run it is this nationalist worship of Gordon that has enabled him to survive. Because of it the bust of Gordon found a place in the Poets' Corner of Westminster Abbey, the only Australian writer to be so honoured. Few critics of today would believe that he deserves that mark of fame.

Henry Kendall has fallen between the two extremes of treatment accorded his fellow colonials, being more popular than Harpur but not as lionized as Gordon. General critical approval of him grew to such an extent in his latter years and immediately after his death that there were many suggestions for recognizing his services to Australian literature — public subscriptions, memorials, honorary degrees and so on. It was the sentimental, wistful landscape lyrist whose services to Australian poetry were so greatly esteemed.

[He was] the first interpreter of the long silent soul of the strange new land which, with a flora, fauna, and a wondrous wealth of its own, had also as wondrous a poetry.[7]

Kendall could do one thing well — he could write sweet verses on serious subjects — he could pour out a perfect luxury of "linked sweetness long-drawn out"; but in prose, in humorous verse, or even in verse that required a dramatic treatment, he was but little above mediocrity.[8]

[He] touched and softened sympathetic hearts with his sweet and melancholy confidences.[9]

With the advent of nationalism his reputation fell away. The nationalists labelled his poetry un-Australian, criticizing him for his lyric mode, his romantic English diction and his obsession with the lush coastal landscapes, the same characteristics that his contemporaries had admired. The darlings of the nationalists — the bush balladists — set their verses, invariably in the ballad meter in language largely colloquial, in the arid outback — which they saw as the real Australia — and peopled them with the outback archetypes — drovers, bullock-drivers, shearers, and squatters. There are signs that Kendall may have been interested in participating in this literary development which Gordon had started (for example, his own poems "Bill the Bullock Driver" and "Jim the Splitter"), but his death in 1882 came before the bush ballad swamped the literary scene. The nationalists regarded Kendall as purely "colonial" and this damned him as derivative and imitative. The critical criteria of the nationalists no longer count for very much, but an unfortunate result of their indictment of Kendall was to continue the emphasis on only one area of his work — his landscape and personal lyrics. This lyric poetry has proved so unsatisfying, in spite of the earlier enthusiasm for it, that Kendall's reputation, so high in the late colonial period, has, in this century, slumped dramatically. And the emphasis on him as a purely lyric poet has been largely responsible for his decline. Most critics of Australian poetry have tacitly accepted the traditional view that Kendall's forté was the lyric, but finding little evidence of any particular lyric talent in him, they have, instead of turning iconoclasts, lost interest in him altogether. They have made little or no attempt to assess the merit of other areas of his remarkably large collection of verse. Even the most modern (and expert) literary opinion has perpetuated this critical imbalance. G. A. Wilkes in *Australian Literature: A Conspectus,* published in 1969, confines his remarks on Kendall to the landscape poems, ignoring the substantial body of narrative, public and satirical poetry. He reiterates the traditional view that "in the wistful, elegiac poem with a woodland setting . . . Kendall finds his characteristic vein" and that his "evocative" treatment of landscape "places" Kendall in his proper literary niche.[10] Judith Wright in *Preoccupations in Australian Poetry,* published in 1965, is critical of Kendall even attempting anything outside the area of the lyric. She accuses him of "weakness in seeking popularity at the expense of rigid poetic honesty. The kind of acclaim he gained from . . . patriotic odes and sententious verses, and from his few attempts at the bush ballads and racing narratives that had given Gordon his celebrity, but which were somewhat outside Kendall's experience and poetic ambit, was corrupting to his poetic gift for it meant that he was forced into sentimental falsities and away from reality and his own imaginative potentiality." She dismisses poems like "The Glen of Arrawatta" and "A Death in the Bush" as "written largely because Harpur had written narrative poems of the bush." The biblical poems she describes as "colourless and unfelt" and can find in few poems outside the lyrics any ring of "genuine feeling."[11]

In spite of such refusals as these to find, or even to look for, evidence of worth in the general body of Kendall's poetry there has been some recent movement toward reappraisal, reflected especially in the work of Inglis Moore and Kramer and Hope. This reappraisal does not deny the significance of Kendall's lyrics but attempts to see them as part, not the whole, of Kendall's contribution to Australian poetry. Kendall is, at best, an erratic lyrist, certainly capable of attractive melody and brilliant descriptive flights but incapable of sustained control over these two lyric talents. His narrative poetry, on the other hand, reveals a fine selective judgment of theme and a controlled but fluent narrative skill. His love poetry throbs with the ache of unfulfillment and his patriotic verses are animated with sincere, bright hopes for Australia. Many of his poems, especially his memorial verses, his public poems and his tart character sketches of fellow Australians, are complementary chronicles of the colonial age in which he lived. Some of his satires are the equal of the best traditional examples of the literary hatchet at work.

What is missing is the one great poem or series of poems to set the seal upon Kendall's literary achievements. It is easy to see, in retrospect, that the opportunity was there. The fragments of "The Australian Shepherd" show that there was, in the mind of the young poet of the 1860s, the idea of a series of poems linked by the theme of life in the rural vastness of this new land. If "A Death in the Bush" and "The Glen of Arrawatta" had been, not isolated narratives, but the opening chapters of an extended verse saga of colonial Australia, then Kendall, today, would stand acknowledged as the founder of Australian poetry, truly "the Monarch of Song in the land."

Such a composition would have required an incredibly sustained effort, enormous self-discipline and singlemindedness. The circumstances of Kendall's life and character — the anxious battle for economic survival, the years of personal worry, the predisposition to melancholy and intemperance — were all against the production of such a magnum opus. But its absence, and even the defects in the poetry he did write, should not debar him from his proper literary recognition. He dwarfs Adam Lindsay Gordon, one of his two colonial rivals. His stature vis-à-vis Harpur is a more complex matter, confusion arising both from the inability of critics to assess Harpur because of corrupt texts and from Kendall's acclaim of the older poet. Some critics have made too much of the master-pupil relationship between the two, ignoring the fact that this relationship began when Kendall was a fledgling poet in his early twenties and Harpur, a man of fifty, was the colony's most established, if not its only, poet. It was natural that Kendall should respect Harpur's achievements and should wish to emulate them, even taking them at that early stage of his career as the model and inspiration of his own poetry.

Kendall, like Harpur and Gordon, is a minor poet in the literary world at large, but in the Australian scene he assumes considerable proportions. He stands clearly as the most substantial poet of the Australian colonial era.

Notes and References

Chapter One

1. An extract from a letter from Samuel Marsden to Thomas Kendall, quoted in Clifford Tolchard, "Thomas Kendall, Australia's Unhappy Pilgrim," *Walkabout* (May, 1967), 32.

2. Swancott's book, *Gosford and the Henry Kendall Country*, was published in 1966. See Bibliography.

3. Kendall's words were: "Let me say a few words about myself. I was born in this colony; and am now in my nineteenth year of age. My education has been neglected — hence you will very likely find that some of these effusions are immature. . . . They recognize me in this country as the 'first Australian poet.' " On the "neglect" of education it may be said that there is no firm indication of formal schooling. Probably there were some beginnings of a formal education in Sydney between 1844 and 1850 when Kendall was 5 - 10 years old. More than likely he attended his father's school in Grafton in 1852, but for only a few months at most. Again there is a possibility of intermittent schooling at Ulladulla and Fairy Meadow between 1852 and 1855. Kendall attributed his education to his father and most of his "bookishness" to his mother, both by inheritance of her romantic nature and some awareness of literature.

4. The forgery apparently occurred October 16, 1847, the *Sydney Morning Herald* listing the offence December 29, 1847, with the report of the trial and sentencing, January 3, 1848. These details are from Donovan Clarke's unpublished thesis, "A Critical Edition of the Letters of Henry Kendall."

5. These details are from Kendall's letter to J. Sheridan Moore, June 29, 1877.

6. Letter to Henry Parkes, October 5, 1863.

7. The *Sydney Morning Herald*, October 24, 1862; the *Goulburn Chronicle*, November 26, 1862; Review by "Iota" (name of newspaper and date missing) in Kendall's Scrap Book in possession of T. T. Reed.

8. *Bulletin*, Red Page (July 9, 1930). Stephens mentions an incident in which Rose Bennett was being farewelled by Kendall at Redfern Station, Sydney. Rose dropped her parasol out of the train window and said, "Pick that up, Harry!" Kendall said, "Say please." She became annoyed and the two parted in ill-temper. This rift widened to a final parting. The story lacks corroboration however.

9. In a brief comment accompanying the publication of "A Death in the Bush" Horne said ... "whatever merits some of the other competitive poems possess . . . they come under the denomination of good 'occasional poems', written by amateurs; while 'Arakoon' [Kendall's pseudonym for the competition] is evidently one who has made Poetry and the Poetic Art, both in reading and writing, the ruling passion of his life. Such poems as 'A Death in the Bush' are produced by no other means, and by no other men; never have been and never will be."

10. This manuscript of G. G. McCrae is in the possession of T. T. Reed.

11. Frances Myers, *Bulletin*, Red Page (September 17, 1903).

12. *My Father and My Father's Friends* (Sydney: Angus & Robertson, 1935), pp 42 - 43.

13. Charles Edward Horsley and Kendall were jointly commissioned for the music and words of the Cantata. The manuscript is preserved in the Library of the Musical Society of Melbourne. The words of the Cantata were included in the program for the opening ceremony.

14. These and other details of Kendall's treatment at the Gladesville Asylum are in Donovan Clarke's "New Light on Henry Kendall," *Australian Literary Studies* 2 (1966), 211 - 13.

15. Letter to Parkes, March 1, 1873.

16. Letter to Holdsworth, April 10, 1873.

17. Letter to Sheridan Moore, May 17, 1876.

18. Donovan Clarke, "New Light on Henry Kendall," *Australian Literary Studies* 2 (1966), 212.

19. Letter to Sheridan Moore, October 23, 1874.

20. Ibid.

21. These remarks are a composite from several letters; to E. B. Docker, October 13, 1875; P. J. Holdsworth, December 2, 1875; Sheridan Moore, May 17 and June 29, 1876; Henry Halloran, May 29, 1878.

22. Letter to Parkes, June 23, 1880.

23. The official letter of instructions to Kendall, dated May 14, 1881, is in the possession of T. T. Reed.

24. Letter to McCrae, August 10, 1881; to Mrs. Harpur, June 29, 1881.

Chapter Two

1. The *Goulburn Chronicle*, November 26, 1862. Special article by an unnamed Sydney correspondent.

2. Review, undated, and with the name of the newspaper missing, in Kendall's Scrap Book in the possession of T. T. Reed.

3. Review undated, and with the name of the newspaper missing, by "Iota," in Kendall's Scrap Book in the possession of T. T. Reed.

4. Frank Hutchinson, "Henry Kendall," *Sydney University Review,* (December, 1882), 442.

5. Letter to Mrs. A. E. Selwyn, January 2, 1864.

6. Letter to Charles Harpur, October 23, 1865.

7. T. T. Reed, *The Poetical Works of Henry Kendall* (Adelaide, Libraries Board of South Australia, 1966), p. 3. All further references to this collection of Kendall's poetry will be abbreviated *Reed.*

8. *Reed,* p. 231.

9. Letter to Mrs. A. E. Selwyn, March 25, 1865.

10. *Reed,* p. 3.

11. *Reed,* p. 14.

12. *Reed,* p. 39.

13. *Reed,* p. 9.

14. *Reed,* p. 26.

15. *Reed,* p. 29.

16. *Reed,* p. 5.

17. *Reed,* p. 32.

18. *Reed,* p. 19.

19. *Reed,* p. 30.

20. *Reed,* p. 43.

21. *Reed,* p. 14.

22. *Reed,* p. 20.

23. *Reed,* p. 32.

24. *Reed,* p. 262 as "A Death Scene in the Bush"; p. 309 as "Orara — A Tale"; p. 84 as "A Death in the Bush."

25. *Reed,* p. 10.

26. *Reed,* p. 24.

27. *Reed,* p. 38

28. *Reed,* p. 90.

29. These extracts are from "Black Lizzie", *Reed,* p. 152; "Peter the Piccaninny," *Reed,* p. 184; "Jack the Blackfellow," *Reed,* p. 423.

30. *Reed,* p. 241.

Chapter Three

1. Alexander Sutherland, "Henry Clarence Kendall," *Melbourne Review* 7 (October, 1882), 400.

2. *Reed,* p. 63.

3. *Reed,* p. 63.

4. Letters dated August 19, 1863; October 26, 1863; August 26, 1865.

5. *Preoccupations in Australian Poetry,* p. 26.

6. *Reed,* p. 83.

7. Quoted in Elizabeth Perkins, "Harpur's Notes and Kendall's 'Bell Birds,'" *Australian Literary Studies* 5 (1972), 112.

8. A. C. W. Mitchell, "The Radiant Dream: Notes on Henry Kendall," *Australian Literary Studies* 4 (1969), 112. Professor James McAuley in his review of T. T. Reed's *The Poetical Works of Henry Kendall* defends Kendall's description of the bellbird's notes. See *Australian Literary Studies* 3 (1968), 314 - 15.

9. *Reed*, p. 66.

10. *Bread and Wine* (Sydney, 1970), p. 87.

11. *Reed*, p. 74.

12. *Reed*, p. 70.

13. *Reed*, p. 101.

14. Kendall wrote (June 5, 1880) to Brunton Stephens commenting on the differences in their respective poetry. He said, "I work in another garden, but the roses that grow in yours are very dear to me. . . . Comparisons in our case are out of place. I am simply a man of the woods. I was born in the forests and the mountains were my sponsors."

15. *Preoccupations in Australian Poetry*, p. 34.

16. *Reed*, pp. 299, 368.

17. *Reed*, pp. 301, 344.

18. *Reed*, pp. 69, 118.

19. Alexander Sutherland, op. cit. 399.

20. T. T. Reed, unpublished thesis, "The Life and Poetical Works of Henry Kendall," (1953), pp 262 - 63.

21. "Australian Poetry to 1920," in Dutton, *The Literature of Australia* (Adelaide: Penguin Books, 1964), p. 66.

22. p. xix.

23. Leonie Kramer and A. D. Hope, *Henry Kendall* (Melbourne: Sun Books, 1973), pp. xxxiii-xxxix. Further references will be abbreviated to *Kramer and Hope*.

24. *Reed*, p. 106.

25. F. W. Watt, Ed., *Matthew Arnold*, New Oxford English Series (London Oxford University Press, 1964), pp. 171, 173.

26. *Reed*, p. 93.

27. *Reed*, p. 103.

28. Frank Hutchinson, op. cit. 442 - 43.

29. Alexander Sutherland, op. cit. 399.

30. *Reed*, p. 383.

31. 2 Kings 21.

32. *Reed*, p. 124.

33. *Reed* gives these variations in full, pp. 127 - 29.

34. *Reed*, p. 366.

35. *Reed*, p. 139.

36. *Reed*, p. 11.

37. *Reed*, p. 112.

38. *Reed*, p. 122.

39. *Reed*, p. 116.

40. *Reed*, p. 347.
41. *Reed*, p. 192.
42. *Reed*, p. 417.
43. *Reed*, p. 100.
44. *Australian Journal*, October, 1869, 10.
45. *Reed*, p. 331.
46. *Reed*, p. 136.
47. *Reed*, p. 351.
48. *Reed*, p. 283.
49. Letter to Mrs. A. E. Selwyn, March 25, 1865.
50. *Reed*, p. 352.
51. *Reed*, p. 371.
52. Gordon, in a letter to Kendall in 1870 wrote — "Your Hut by the Black Swamp is glorious. I never read it before; now I know it by heart."

Chapter Four

1. The letters to Holdsworth were dated July 14 and September 14, 1874.
2. Letters to William Maddock, December 12 and December 17, 1880.
3. Alexander Sutherland, 407.
4. Letter to G. G. McCrae, October 2, 1880.
5. These poems are not included in *Reed*.
6. *Reed*, p. 160.
7. *Reed*, p. 170.
8. *Reed*, p. 27.
9. *Reed*, p. 170.
10. Letter to Holdsworth, July 14, 1874.
11. *Reed*, p. 187.
12. *Reed*, p. 160.
13. *Reed*, p. 192.
14. *Reed*, p. 417.
15. *Reed*, p. 202.
16. *Reed*, p. 226.
17. *Reed*, p. 333.
18. Published in the *Australian Journal*, October, 1869. Reproduced in *Kramer and Hope*, p. 93.
19. Not included in *Reed*. See *Kramer and Hope*, p. 53.
20. Letter to Fagan, June 3, 1879.
21. Letter to Halloran, June 3, 1879.
22. Letter to Parkes, February 18, 1880.
23. See Inglis Moore, op. cit., p. 161.
24. Letter to Parkes, February 19, 1866.
25. Letter to Parkes, August 5, 1869.
26. *Reed*, p. 432.
27. *Reed*, p. 165.
28. *Reed*, p. 156.

29. Letter to Thomas Butler, January 23, 1880.

30. *Reed*, p. 173.

31. From Lawson's poem, "Middleton's Rousabout."

32. *Reed*, p. 193.

33. *Reed*, p. 143.

34. *Preoccupations in Australian Poetry*, p. 46.

35. *Kramer and Hope*, pp. xvi, xvii.

Chapter Five

1. "Men of Letters in New South Wales," *Punch Staff Papers* (1872). Quoted in *Kramer and Hope*, p. 123.

2. "Notes Upon Men and Books. No. 3 — Walt Whitman," *Freeman's Journal*, December 16, 1871. Quoted in *Kramer and Hope*, pp. 96 - 103.

3. "Men of Letters in New South Wales and Victoria", *Freeman's Journal*, March 2, 1872. Quoted in *Kramer and Hope*, p. 112.

4. This, and the following extract, are from *Punch Staff Papers* (1872). Quoted in *Kramer and Hope*, pp. 118 - 125.

5. These extracts and those following from "Old Manuscripts" are in *Freeman's Journal* November 17, 1877, p. 17.

6. "The August Windeyer," *Freeman's Journal*, February 9, 1878. p. 13.

7. "Jones — A Biography — By the Mopoke," *Freeman's Journal*, October 19, 1880. Quoted in *Kramer and Hope*, p. 145.

8. "Arcadia in our midst," *Town and Country Journal*, February 23, March 6, 1875.

9. "My New Home," *Town and Country Journal*, May 5, 1881.

10. "Their Literary and Historical Importance," Chapter 7, p. 2.

11. This letter was written to Mrs. Selwyn, the wife of Rev. A. E. Selwyn, who had apparently lent money to Kendall in 1864. Letter dated March 25, 1865.

12. Judith Wright, *Charles Harpur* (Melbourne, 1963), p. 24.

13. Letter to Harpur, April 29, 1865.

Chapter Six

1. Kenneth Slessor, *Bread and Wine* (Sydney, 1970), p. 81.

2. The epitaph, written in pencil, is with the Stenhouse papers. J. Normington-Rawling, who quotes the epitaph in *Charles Harpur, An Australian* (Sydney, 1962), p. 297, is unaware of how it got there.

3. A. P. Martin, "Two Australian Poets," *Melbourne Review* 5 (1880), 448.

4. Alexander Sutherland, "Adam Lindsay Gordon, Australian Poet," *Once A Month* 2 (1885), 245.

5. J. W. L., "Some Aspects of Gordon's Poetry," *Alma Mater* 2 (1900); *Bulletin*, Red Page (December 12, 1912); Judith Wright, *Preoccupations in Australian Poetry* (Melbourne, 1965), p. 57.

6. An extract from a letter written by Barcroft Boake to his father, November 20, 1889. Boake was, at the time, droving out of Cunnamulla and in close contact with the "Backblockers" whose opinions he was quoting.

7. Frank Hutchinson, op. cit., 441.

8. Alexander Sutherland, op. cit., 397.

9. W. B. Dalley, "Henry Kendall," the *Sydney Mail* (August 12, 1882) 431.

10. p. 26.

11. pp. 28 - 29.

Selected Bibliography

PRIMARY SOURCES

1. Manuscripts

a) Mitchell Library, Sydney.
Letters. Catalog Nos. C199, A68, D19, Am38. Letters from Kendall (holograph) to various correspondents from 1862 to 1882. Correspondents include Charles Harpur, J. Sheridan Moore, N. D. Stenhouse, Henry Parkes, P. J. Holdsworth, J. Brunton Stephens, Rev. A. E. Selwyn, Mrs. Selwyn, Anne Hopkins.
Poems. Catalog No. C198. Twenty-eight poems in Kendall's handwriting. Seven poems of Kendall's in Mrs. Kendall's handwriting. Kendall's own copy of *Poems and Songs*, 1862, revised and corrected in his own hand with comments on certain poems.
Newspaper cuttings. Catalog Nos. 991, 8M, Q991.N. Reminiscences and recollections of Kendall by contemporaries from various areas of New South Wales where the poet and his family had lived.
b) National Library, Canberra.
Poems. Three notebooks containing poems by Kendall in his own handwriting. Some fair copies; most have deletions and corrections.
Vol. 1 August 15, 1877 - October 21, 1879. 29 poems
Vol. 2 November 26, 1879 - June 18, 1880. 19 poems
Vol. 3 July 29, 1880 - February 27, 1881. 14 poems
Miscellaneous matter in these notebooks includes also lecture notes, comments on poems, list of subscribers to *Songs from the Mountains*.
c) Archbishop Reed's Collection
Letters. (1) Fifty-nine letters from Kendall to Henry Halloran, G. G. McCrae, Thomas Butler, Mostly copies from originals.
(2) Letters from Kendall (holograph) to Miss Charlotte Rutter, who

became his wife and letters to Miss Rutter's brothers from Kendall. These letters concern the periods immediately before and after his marriage in 1868 and immediately before the reunion of Kendall and his wife in the 1870s.

(3) About one hundred and fifty letters to Kendall from 1862 onward. Correspondents include Charles Harpur, N. D. Stenhouse, J. L. Michael, Basil Edward Kendall, W. B. Dalley, Henry Halloran, Henry Parkes.

Miscellaneous. (1) Kendall's Scrap Books, kept by him from 1862 to his death. Press cuttings etc.

(2) Scrap Books by Mrs. Kendall containing cuttings about death of her husband and the memorial to him.

(3) Frederick C. Kendall's recollections of his parents.

(4) Material formerly in possession of the Fagan family, for example, manuscripts of two poems and two lectures, various letters.

d) Unpublished theses

Clark, Donovan C. "A Critical Edition of the Letters of Henry Kendall." For the degree of M.A., Sydney University, 1959.

Reed, T. T. "The Life and Poetical Works of Henry Kendall." For the degree of Doctor of Letters, University of Adelaide, 1953.

2. Texts (Arranged chronologically)

Silent Tears. Sydney: Peck's Music Repository. 1859. Words by Henry Kendall, music by George Peck. Two editions of this song were published, the second edition in 1860. There are no known extant copies.

Poems and Songs. Sydney: J. R. Clarke; London: Sampson, Low, Son and Marston, 1862.

"At Long Bay: Euroclydon." Sydney, c. 1865. Two poems on a single sheet, folio, undated. No imprint. One copy in Mitchell Library, Sydney.

"The Glen of the Whiteman's Grave." Sydney: Hanson and Bennett, 1865. The booklet of eight pages, including also the poem "Cui Bono?", is undated but reference was made to it in *Sydney Punch*, October 7, 1865. Reprinted in *Leaves from Australian Forests*, 1869, as "The Glen of Arrawatta"; republished, with some variations, additions and engravings, as "Orara" Melbourne: Art Union of Victoria, 1881.

"The Bronze Trumpet." A Satirical Poem by*. Sydney, 1866. No imprint. Dedicated to "The Shams, Political, Clerical and Critical, of Sydney, and (in particular) to the Puny Punsters of Punch." Referred to in *Sydney Punch*, January 13, 1866. Although anonymous, strong evidence points to Kendall as the author (For example, in letter to Charles Harpur, December 2, 1865).

Prince Alfred's Wreath: A Collection of Australian Poems by various Authors. Edited by W. H. H. Yarrington. Sydney: A. W. Douglas, 1868. Includes "In Hyde Park" and "Australia Vindex."

Leaves From Australian Forests. Melbourne: George Robertson, 1869. Some copies dated 1870 may have been produced in England or in a second binding in Australia.

Williams's Illustrated Australian Annual for Christmas and the New Year. Melbourne: W. H. Williams, 1868 - 69, 1869 - 70. The 1868 - 69 edition contains Kendall's poem "A Death in the Bush." The 1869 - 70 Edition contains his "Orara — A Fragment" and "The Native Wren."

"Euterpe: An Ode to Music." Melbourne, 1870. Printed in the program of the Festival to celebrate the opening of the Melbourne Town Hall, August 9, 1870. Music of the cantata is by C. E. Horsley.

"Honor the Hero." Sydney, 1872. Song, words by Kendall, set to music by C. S. Packer. Single sheet, octavo, no imprint, undated.

Punch Staff Papers: A Collection of Tales, Sketches etc. by the Members of the Staff of "Sydney Punch." Sydney: Gordon and Gotch, 1872. Includes Kendall's "Sedan" (printed in the *Sydney Morning Herald* July 2, 1863, as "England Aloof"); "Aboriginal Death Song"; "*To* . . . . ." (that is, "To My Brother Basil E. Kendall"); "Death of Acis" (published in *Songs from the Mountains* as "Galatea"); "Basil Moss" and "Sydney Harbour."

"In Memoriam: Nicol Drysdale Stenhouse." Single sheet. No date or imprint. c. 1873. Stenhouse died February 18, 1873.

"Something to His Advantage: An Australian Christmas Serial." Edited by Richmond Thatcher. Sydney: Turner and Henderson, 1875. Includes Kendall's "Christmas in England and Australia."

"Our Exhibition Annual." Edited by H. W. H. Stephen. Sydney: J. J. Moore, 1878. Includes Kendall's "Hosee's Gully" better known by the title "Cooranbean" used in *Songs from the Mountains*, 1880.

Cantata. Written expressly for the opening ceremony of the Sydney International Exhibition. Words by Kendall, music by Giorza. Published by the Composer. Sydney, 1879.

Melbourne Christmas Annual: Stories and Verse. Melbourne: A. H. Massina and Company, 1880. Includes Kendall's "Christmas Creek" and "Christmas in the Splitters' Camp."

Songs From the Mountains. Sydney: W. Maddock; London: Sampson, Low, Marston, Searle and Rivington, 1880. The original edition contained "The Song of Ninian Melville" on pages 144 - 152. The publisher, W. Maddock, believing the political satire to be possibly libellous, suppressed the edition after some 250 copies had been distributed. The satire was excised and replaced by "Christmas Creek." The book reappeared in January, 1881.

"Orara." Melbourne: Art Union of Victoria, 1881. The revised version of "The Glen of Arrawatta" (51 lines added). In addition to the text there are thirteen lithographed engravings by various artists.

Australian Stories in Prose and Verse. Melbourne: Cameron Laing, 1882. Includes Kendall's "Hunted Down" and "Wamberal."

"The Song of Ninian Melville." Edited by J. Whitley. Sydney, 1885. No imprint. Another edition was published about 1903 (no date) by Times Printing Works, Parramatta.

Poems of Henry Kendall, Edited by Alexander Sutherland (anonymously)

with a prefatory note by P. J. Holdsworth. Melbourne: George
Robertson and Company, 1866. First collected edition. 100 poems.
Poems of Henry Clarence Kendall. Edited with a Memoir by Alexander
Sutherland. Melbourne: George Robertson and Company, 1890. 96
poems.
Poems of Henry Clarence Kendall. Revised and enlarged edition by
Frederick C. Kendall. Melbourne: George Robertson and Company
Pty. Ltd., 1903. 114 poems.
Poems. Miniature Edition. Melbourne: Thomas C. Lothian, 1910.
The Poems of Henry Kendall. Edited with a Biographical Note, by Bertram
Stevens. Sydney: Angus and Robertson, 1920. 224 poems.
Selected Poems of Henry Kendall. Edited with Preface and Memoir, by
Frederick C. Kendall. Sydney: Angus and Robertson, 1923. 65 poems.
A Wild Night. Melbourne: Lee and Kaye, undated. Kendall's "God Help
our Men at Sea" set to music by G. B. Allen.
Rose Lorraine and Other Poems. Sydney: W. H. Honey Publishing Com-
pany. Undated but appeared in 1945.
Selected Poems of Henry Kendall. Edited, with biographical and critical in-
troduction by T. Inglis Moore. Sydney: Angus and Robertson, 1957.
Australian Poets: Henry Kendall. Selection and introduction by T. Inglis
Moore. Sydney: Angus and Robertson, 1963. Australian Poets Series.
The Poetical Works of Henry Kendall. Edited with introduction and notes
by T. T. Reed, Bishop of Adelaide. Adelaide: Libraries Board of South
Australia, 1966. Definitive edition, including ninety hitherto un-
collected poems, but excluding several satires such as "The Gagging
Bill," "The Sawyer Who Works on the Top," and "A Psalm for the
Conventicle." Appendices include examples of the verse of Melinda
Kendall, the poet's mother, and of Basil Edward Kendall, his twin
brother.
Henry Kendall. Edited by Leonie Kramer and A. D. Hope. Introduction by
A. D. Hope. Melbourne, Sun Books Pty. Ltd., 1973. Published with
the assistance of the Commonwealth Literary Fund. *Three Colonial
Poets* series. A selection chosen particularly to substantiate the
authors' critical view that Kendall's narrative poetry is superior to his
lyric strain. A valuable addition to Kendall criticism.

SECONDARY SOURCES

1. Books

DUTTON, GEOFFREY, ed. *The Literature of Australia.* Adelaide: Penguin
Books, 1964. See "Australian Poetry to 1920," pp. 55 - 99 by Judith
Wright. An examination of the relationship between Harpur and Kendall. Stresses Kendall's lyric poetry, dismissing his patriotic and
biblical verse. See "The Colonial Poets," pp. 227 - 46 by Brian Elliott.

Biographical details of Kendall. Discusses Kendall's poetic ambitions and his failure to achieve them.

ELLIOTT, BRIAN. *The Landscape of Australian Poetry*. Melbourne: F. W. Chesire, 1967. See "Channels of Coolness", pp. 100 - 19. Kendall's projection of himself into his landscape poetry. Criticism of the imagery in the landscape poetry.

GREEN, H. M. *Fourteen Minutes*. Sydney: Angus and Robertson, 1930. A book of "radio" talks on Australian poets, one talk being on Kendall. Useful general but superficial discussion.

HAMILTON-GREY, A. M. *The Poet Kendall: His Romantic History*. Sydney: Sands, 1926.

———. *Kendall: Our God-Made Chief, A Singer of the Dawn*. Sydney: Sands, 1929. Highly colored and individualistic interpretations of Kendall's life and times.

HOPE, A. D. *Native Companions: Perspectives in Australian Literature*. Sydney: Angus & Robertson, 1974. Examination of three early Australian poets, Wentworth, Harpur and Kendall. Hope admires Kendall's narrative poems and sees links with Matthew Arnold and Swinburne.

KENDALL, FREDERICK C. *Henry Kendall — His Later Years: A Refutation of Mrs. Hamilton-Grey's Book, "Kendall — Our God-Made Chief"* Sydney: Sands, 1938.

McCRAE, HUGH. *My Father and My Father's Friends*. Sydney: Angus and Robertson, 1935. Some personal comments on Kendall by his contemporary, George Gordon McCrae.

PRINGLE, J. B. *On Second Thoughts: Australian Essays*, Sydney: Angus and Robertson, 1971. See "A Death on the Clarence" pp. 134 - 49. Deals mainly with J. L. Michael but interesting because of Kendall's relationship with him.

REED, T. T. *Henry Kendall: A Critical Appreciation*. Adelaide: Rigby, 1960. Valuable biographical material and commentary on background to Kendall's poetry.

SLESSOR, KENNETH. *Bread and Wine*. Sydney: Angus and Robertson, 1970. See "Kendall and Gordon" pp. 75 - 91 and "Australian Poetry: Sonnet and Ballad" pp. 127 - 47. Highly critical analysis of Kendall's well-known lyric poems and a commentary on such "guilt" poems as "On a Street" and "At Her Window."

SWANCOTT, CHARLES. *Gosford and the Henry Kendall Country*. Woy Woy: New South Wales, The Author, 1966. Description of the Brisbane Water country and a somewhat fictional account of Kendall's activities there, 1873 - 74.

WRIGHT, JUDITH. *Preoccupations in Australian Poetry*. Melbourne: Oxford University Press, 1965. See "Henry Kendall," pp. 20 - 46. Discusses the influence of Harpur's poetry on Kendall, the problems Kendall

faced in the materialistic colonial environment, Kendall's landscape
poems, the importance of "To a Mountain."

2. Articles in Periodicals

CLARKE, DONOVAN. "Henry Kendall — A Study in Imagery," *Australian
Quarterly*, 29 pt. 4 (1957) 71 - 79; 30 pt. 1 (1958) 89 - 98. Traces
decline of Kendall's literary reputation. Pt. 1 examines imagery and
symbolism in Poems and Songs; pt. 2 does the same for the later
volumes.

————. "Kendall's Views on Contemporary Writers: A Survey of His
Correspondence," *Australian Literary Studies* 1 (1964) 170 - 79. Ken-
dall's critical views of fellow Australian poets Harpur, G. G. McCrae,
Gordon and English poets Tennyson, Rossetti and others.

————. "New Light on Henry Kendall," *Australian Literary Studies* 2
(1966) 211 - 13. Biographical details of years 1870 - 73, for example,
Kendall's treatment at Gladesville Mental Asylum.

DALLEY, W. B. "Henry Kendall," the *Sydney Mail*, (August 12, 1882) 430 -
33. Memorial eulogy emphasizing sadness of Kendall's life and the
reflection of this in his poetry.

DUTTON, GEOFFREY. "Australian Poetic Diction," Australian Letters 1, no. 1
(1957) 12 - 16. Reprinted in *Twentieth Century Australian Literary
Criticism*, ed. C. Semmler (Melbourne: Oxford University Press,
1967). The qualities of Kendall's descriptive language.

HOPE, A. D. "Henry Kendall: a Dialogue with the Past," *Southerly* 22
(1972) 163 - 73. Kendall's efforts to "acclimatize" Australian poetry.
His affiliations with Wordsworth. Influences on Kendall's lyric
poetry. Kendall's satires as evidence of him as a "social poet." Praise
of Kendall's narrative poems.

HUTCHINSON, F. "Henry Kendall," *Sydney University Review* (October,
1882) 388 - 410. Biographical information. Critical of Kendall's
classical poems and sonnets. Emphasis on the lyrics. Kendall
described as Australia's "Morning Star of Song."

MITCHELL, A. C. W. "The Radiant Dream: Notes on Henry Kendall,"
Australian Literary Studies 4 (1969) 99 - 114. Examines Kendall's
poetry for a system of imagery and the functions of the imagery in his
poems.

MOORE, T. INGLIS. "Henry Kendall in a Bibliography," *Biblionews* 10 (1957)
6 - 9.

PERKINS, ELIZABETH. "Harpur's 'Notes' and Kendall's 'Bell Birds,' "
Australian Literary Studies 5 (1972) 277 - 84. Discusses the language
connections between the extensive notes supplied by Harpur with his
poem "The Kangaroo or a Morning in the Mountains" and Kendall's
poem "Bell Birds."

SALIER, C. W. "Harpur and Kendall. Footnotes to a Friendship," *Southerly* 9 (1948) 101 - 08. Examines the similarity in themes of the two poets, especially the links between Harpur's "The Creek of the Four Graves" and Kendall's "The Glen of Arrawatta."

SMITH, LILLIAN A. "By Channels of Coolness," *Walkabout*, 20 no. 4 (1954) 41 - 42. Biographical details of Kendall's stay at Gosford, 1873 - 74, with quotations from "Mooni," "Narrara Creek" and "Names Upon a Stone."

STEPHENS, A. G. "Henry Kendall," *Bookfellow* (December 15, 1919). Reprinted in *Twentieth Century Australian Criticism*, ed. C. Semmler (Melbourne: Oxford University Press, 1967), pp. 147 - 48. Brief commentary only.

———. "Kendalliana," *Bulletin*, Red Page, (July 9, 1930). Some details of the Kendall - Rose Bennett love affair.

SUTHERLAND, A. "Henry Clarence Kendall," *Melbourne Review*, 7 (October, 1882), 388 - 410. Exaggerated praise of Kendall's verse, comparing him with Wordsworth and Milton. Much biographical material.

TOLCHARD, CLIFFORD. "Henry Kendall at Gosford," *Walkabout*, 29, no. 10 (1963) 20 - 22. Fictionalized account of Kendall's stay with the Fagan family at Narara Creek.

WILLIAMS, T. L. "Henry Kendall: A National Australian Poet," *Journal of the Royal Queensland Historical Society*, 8 (1967) 388 - 96. Emphasis on the role of Kendall as a native Australian poet.

Index

177